GEORGE A. SIPL

My Life In Rock and Roll

UNDERSTATED

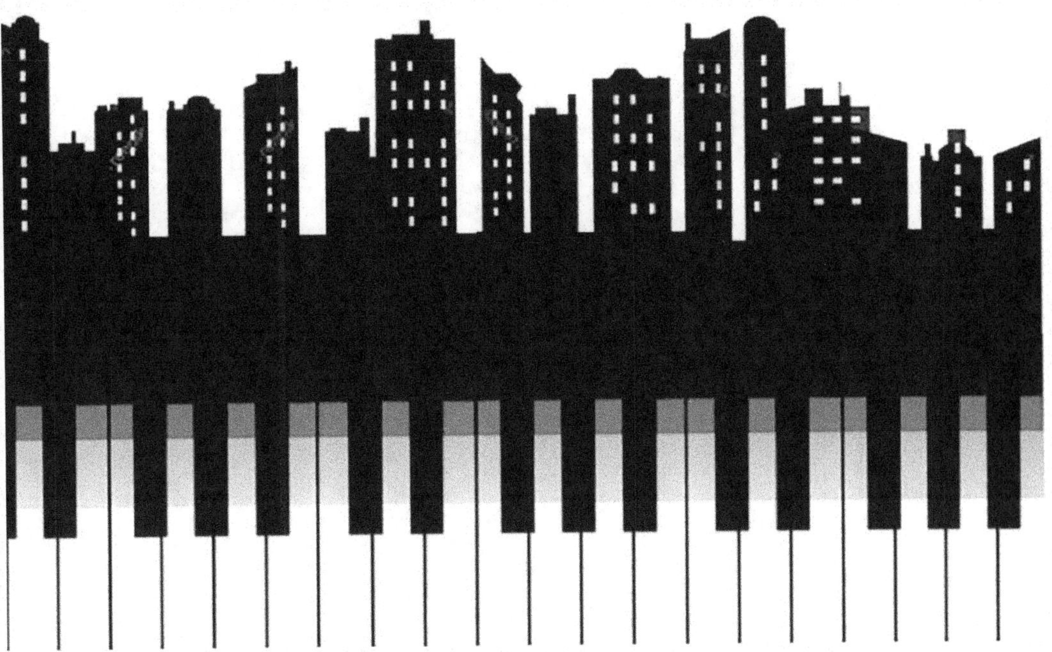

Oral History by George A. Sipl
Written by Janet Sipl

Content

<u>Forward</u>

You may ask, "Why this book?" Well, you can blame it on my wife, Janet. She wanted to write a relatable, inspirational story that her middle school students would be interested in reading. She wanted it to show how a young person can overcome adversity; and with spirit and hard work they can still fulfill their dreams. To my surprise, she said that was me.

She felt that since my life went from playing the piano before I could read, to then cutting off three fingers of my right hand, I definitely had the adversity down.

She also said I had the spirit and hard work she was looking for because I didn't give up. Even though I had cut my fingers off, I still went on to major in music (piano) in college; and ultimately went on to perform on stage and tour with Eric Carmen.

All-in-all she said, "It was an amazing story that needed to be told." So, I said, "OK, as long as you do the writing." And if you are reading this now, she did write it and the rest is history. The book is done.

The book is unique in the fact that I conveyed my life's journey orally to Janet. She would tape our conversations and take notes. She would then painstakingly type my thoughts, feelings and adventures into "book speak language," so that everyone would understand what I was trying to say.

So here it is with humor and love, as told by me and written down by Janet.

Acknowledgements

I want to acknowledge my family and friends, my mentors, instructors and respected colleagues. From those who believed in me, to those who inspired me or pushed me to become the best me I could be, you have made ordinary moments in my life extraordinary.

To the love of my life, Janet.
She is definitely my *"Rock"* while I *"Roll"*!

A special thank you to my publishing team:
Karin Komar – Editing, Proofreading
Krista Smith-Rasmussen – Proofreading
Michael Gerard Szalkowski – Final Proof
Charlie Wiener – Formatting
Janet Sipl – Author, Editor

To Lil' Miss and Lil' Bit –For the love and happiness our adorable westies bring into our lives. Our world would not be the same without them.

<u>Preface</u>

HOW I GOT HERE

全全全

The path to the present wasn't always straight forward. It was more like a maze. Much like the one in the movie *The Shining*. Not as cold, but at times just as scary. Throughout my journey I would periodically hit a wall and find myself at a standstill. I then had a choice. I could stay where I was, go left, right or even backtrack if I had to. I knew I would have to make adjustments or even add a new skill because I would never stay stagnant and give up on my dreams. Making changes allowed me to continue forward, just by way of an alternate path.

During my journey, I have had to constantly adapt, change and reinvent myself. But this is not a negative. It has allowed me to identify potential opportunities I may never have known.

I am not a flashy or a self-important person. But on the other hand, I don't put my self-worth in the hands of others. I am just quietly confident about my role in life, understated in a manner of speaking. Hence the name of the book.

Now that I am older, I've come to realize that my ultimate goals have always been happiness, fulfillment and time to do what I love, with those I love. Music and creativity have just been tools to get me too those goals. They were never an end in themselves.

They say it takes a village to raise a child. Well, that is also true for a musician. I have had the love and support of many people in my life including those mentioned in this book. I am happy with who I am and with what I have accomplished, but I'm not done yet.

***

So, here is my story. I will only share events that are relevant and actually took place. I am not a psychologist, so I can only attest to my own mindset on any specific event. I will share experiences as I remember them from my point of view. Drawing conclusions, I'll leave to the reader.

I hope you enjoy reading about my life. It was a blast living it!

1

IN THE BEGINNING

仝仝仝

Some might think being a first born American of German descent would be a disadvantage to becoming successful in America, but much to the contrary. Instead, it has instilled in me an undeniable drive and work ethic and the capacity to dream a dream and keep working until I have achieved it. Here is the story behind that drive and work ethic.

***

Tito, who was the dictator of Yugoslavia hated anyone of German descent. It did not matter that these German families and their ancestors had lived in Yugoslavia for over a hundred years. During World War II, Tito and his brutal partisan army came at gunpoint to my parent's village in Yugoslavia, and they didn't hold back their attack dogs. They confiscated all the land, homes and worldly possessions of anyone of German descent. At the time there were only women, children and the elderly still living in the village. All the men including my father had been taken away, forced to serve in the army.

Tito's Partisans ruthlessly forced all of these German women, children and the elderly, including my mother, sister (Anna), brother (Michael), maternal grandmother (Oma) and my dad's father to march at gunpoint to Gakowa, the Forced Labor Internment Camp in Yugoslavia. Many died along the way.

My mother had two children but she was still young herself. She was only twenty-eight, but she felt her age was an advantage and would give them a fighting chance. She was determined to survive and get her family through this. My mother was now the core that held the family together.

Everyone in the camp had their heads shaved because of lice. They separated families into worker and non-worker barracks. The non-workers consisted mostly of the elderly and the sick. Most everyone in the non-working group did not survive the conditions at the camp. My grandfather was one of them. He did not survive. He was hurriedly buried just where he died, in a ditch next to the railroad tracks.

My mother, sister, grandmother and even my brother who had leg braces because of having polio, worked in the fields. This was important because workers would sometimes be given slices of old dry bread to share. My mother would moisten it in warm water to make it edible. They would boil roots of plants to make a broth or even gather the maggots from the officer's garbage dump and cook them to eat. Maggots were a good source of protein. My mother had to disguise them so my sister Anna would eat them. It was hard for my mom to watch food being brought in for the officers who ran the camp when so many prisoners were starving to death. Yet, even with all the odds stacked against them, my mother, grandmother, sister and brother did survive to be reunited with my father after the war. It is this determination and work ethic that I inherited.

***

I was born in Sharon, Pennsylvania in 1953, shortly after my parents, Michael, Anna, and my grandmother Oma arrived in the United States. The war had taken everything from them, family members, friends and all their worldly possessions. Having no money and not speaking the language in a new country would have been a scary prospect for anyone to face, but for my family it was just another mountain to climb.

I remember my mother telling me about their first Halloween in America. They had just come to the United States. They didn't know anyone, speak any English or understand any of the customs. So, when the first group of kids escorted by their parents came banging at their door yelling, "Trick or Treat," my mother took Oma, my brother and sister and hid in the basement. Flashes of Tito's Partisans were running through her head.

It was not until my dad came home and explained what was going on that she finally felt safe enough to come out of hiding. It took some time, but finally everyone settled in and focused on building their new life and pursuing the great American dream.

We spoke mostly German at home. As a result, I learned a large part of my everyday vernacular in school by interacting with friends and from that great American educational tool, the television.

Now, you may be snickering, but just think about it. Television presented a cross section of American culture and language. As a child, I consumed this information with interest. From sitcoms to commercials, it helped me develop my English skills while it exposed me to the various cultures of America. So yes, it may have been a peculiar learning tool but from my perspective it was an effective and entertaining one.

In 1955 after changing locations a few times, our family finally put down roots on the west side of Cleveland, Ohio. To this day, I am still a west side boy. I now live in the beautiful suburb of Middleburg Heights on the southwest side of Cleveland. But near or far, once a west side boy always a west side boy.

The west side home my parents purchased was a modest two-story colonial. It was in an average suburban neighborhood on Fortune Avenue in Cleveland. It had parks to play in and the schools were nearby. It wasn't exactly a Norman Rockwell painting but it was our home. We felt safe and were prospering. There was no money for trendy extras, just enough to make ends meet and have a little savings. My mother had a vegetable garden and my dad would handle all the repairs. As always, they were self-sufficient and relied on no one for handouts.

Despite their language barrier, both my mother and father worked. My dad even had a second job so he could save a little for the future. He had a dream of building his own brick home. But for now, our current home was not brick and was furnished with second-hand furniture. It may never have made the cover of Architectural Digest but it was always neat and immaculately clean. Needless to say, my mother worked as a cleaning lady and my father was a bricklayer.

When we moved into this "not quite a Norman Rockwell home" in Cleveland, the previous owner had left an old upright piano. It was out of tune, had a few non-functioning keys and the ones that did play had a soft spongy feel to them. Who would want such a piece of junk? Well, we did. So, this piano was added to our musical family.

My dad was able to fix the broken keys and have the piano tuned and my mom found just the right spot for it in our front room. Now that old piano stood ready and waiting for someone to play it.

My dad played the guitar and my brother played the accordion, and now we had this piano. My brother easily picked up playing the piano because of its likeness to the accordion and my sister started taking piano lessons.

As an inquisitive two-year-old, I was drawn to this massive object that now resided in our home. I would relentlessly press each ivory key and was fascinated by the sound it would produce. Before long, I made an association between which key made what sound. I realized that the sounds went from low to high in a specific order. This seemed logical to me and it gave me a structured pattern that made perfect sense. It was this realization that changed everything for me. If I heard a note I could find and play it on the keyboard, and when I hit multiple keys at the same time the sound was melodic. Those ivory keys were no longer a mystery.

I continued experimenting and learning but to me it was still just playtime. It was something that was easy and fun to do. By the age of four I figured out how to replicate some popular children's songs on the piano. I was even able to play the smash hit *Catch a Falling Star* by Perry Como.

That certainly was a different time when it came to hit songs.

Those young years with the piano were both formative and magical. I spent my days playing outside with friends and discovering my passion for music.

Before I knew it, it was time to start school. It was 1958 and I was now five years old. I was genuinely excited to start my new adventure in kindergarten. My English was becoming fluent and all my neighborhood friends would be in my class.

Going to school was exciting and fun. I would learn something new and interesting every day and I got to play with my friends. There was even a piano in the classroom. How could it get any better?

My year in Kindergarten at Wilber Wright Elementary School was not only fun but it was a year of growth for me. By year's end I spoke like any other kid born in America.

The year went by quickly. Before I knew it my first year of school was done and I was on summer vacation. I again filled my days doing what I loved best, riding my bike, playing outside with my friends and of course, enjoying the piano.

Image1: **Mom and Dad's Marriage,** Yugoslavia, 1939.

Image 2: **Photos taken at Gakowa Forced Labor Internment Camp**, in Yugoslavia.

Image 3: **Drawing done while in camp.**

Image 4: **My first Birthday,** in front of the old upright piano that was left in the house. Played *Catch a Falling Star* on it at age four.

Image 5: **House on Fortune Avenue**, Cleveland Ohio.

2

A PASSION FOR MUSIC

全全全

Next came first grade at Saints Phillip and James School. Our teacher was Miss Joan. She was young, pretty, and very patient. She made each of us feel special. All the kids loved her and so did I.

Halfway through the school year, Miss Joan brought me home. I thought I was in bigtrouble.

Instead, Miss Joan told my mom, "George should be taking piano lessons, because he is playing every song that I play on the classroom piano, and just by hearing me play them." She continued, "I have never seen anything like it. It's absolutely amazing."

I was only six years old and that's when the years of piano lessons began. But at the time, I was just happy I wasn't in trouble with Miss Joan. Little did I know that these events would be the start of an all-consuming passion for music, and lead me to write this book, *Understated, My Life in Rock and Roll*.

So, as a young boy I was not only learning to read and write in English, but I was learning to read and play music. It would seem a daunting task for any six-year-old, but for me the music flowed easily and felt as natural as breathing. When I heard music, I would automatically visualize it in my head, and be able to transfer that vision of sound to keys on a piano.

Playing the piano came easily but the structured lessons and practice were a battle. Don't get me wrong, I loved the piano, but I also wanted to be outside playing sports with my friends. My parents however, had forbidden me from playing any team sports for fear of hurting my hands. They were paying for the piano lessons, so their rules were law and I had to respect that.

For seven years I took piano lessons and it wasn't always fun. I remember my older sister grabbing me by the ear to make me practice some Stephen Foster or Irving Berlin piece. I think she just liked tormenting me. It's not that I didn't like that kind of music, it's just that I was now thirteen years old and I had discovered rock and roll.

***

It was now 1966. We moved into the beautiful brick home my dad built on Kuenzer Drive in Seven Hills, Ohio. It made me realize that dreams do come true when you work hard to attain them. Our family was now prospering and truly living the American dream.

Joe my baby brother was born and my older sister got married and had a little girl, Bridget. So, while everyone was happy and busy with family and the move, I took the opportunity to quit my piano lessons. I now could focus on what I really wanted to do, which was to play rock and roll music.

Both images **Fortune Avenue, Cleveland, Ohio**
Image 7: Above: **My first bike,** with the Fortune Ave. gang!

Image 8: Below: **My Cub Scout Badges**
Absolutely no sports allowed!

Image 9: **Neighborhood boys from Kuenzer Drive**.
Leonard Corsi, me, Bob Krenkel, John Lauber, Joe Lauber.

Image 10: **The house my dad built.**
Kuenzer Drive, Seven Hills, Ohio.

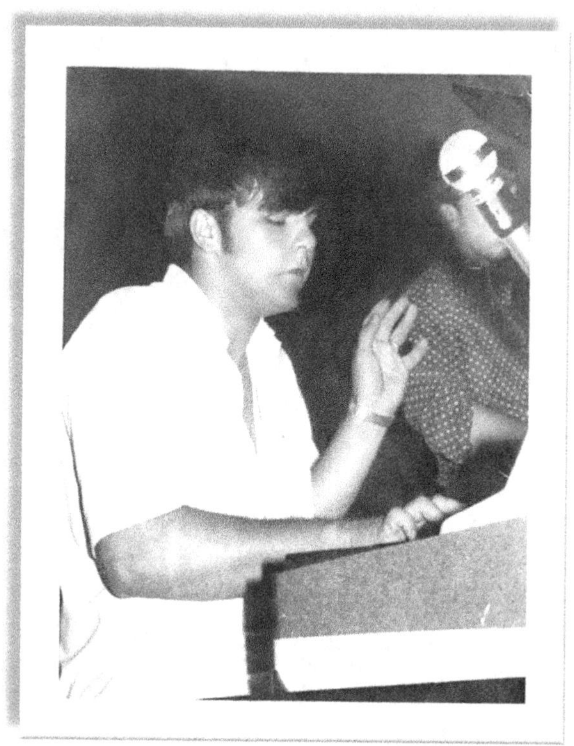

Image 10A: **Playing rock and roll,** Kuenzer Drive, Seven Hills, Ohio.

3

STANDING ROOM ONLY

仝仝仝

It was here in my new neighborhood that I met my best friend of over sixty years Ed Sarley, and his brother Greg. They lived only a few houses down from me and they had a band called Standing Room Only. I was beyond excited. They actually asked me to join their band. The problem was I had no money to buy a portable keyboard, so Ed taught me how to play his guitar and the electric bass.

The band which included Alan Chupa, Ed and Greg Sarley, Jim Stamper and myself was fairly successful. We actually performed at school dances. I was too young to drive, so my dad would take me to and from the gigs.

It wasn't long before Ed and I were recording music in my garage. My dad had this stereo recorder with sound on sound. We experimented with overdubbing tracks, and we recorded some dynamite Beatles songs. I do remember being quite impressed with ourselves. Later in life I wondered if this interaction had been a hint of what would materialize in my future. But for now, my life was playing rock music on stage.

The transition from playing classical music to playing in a rock band could have been tricky; but with Ed's guidance I absorbed the new information like a sponge.

I was now ready to focus on getting some equipment I could use on stage. I purchased a Farfisa Combo Compact organ and a small Vox amp. I was really moving up in the world!

Over the years Standing Room Only went through various metamorphoses including shortening its name to SRO. They expanded, changed members and grew in popularity. The band now consisted of Frank Barrett, Jim Stamper, Mark Ferry, Rich Reising, myself, and later on Steve Knill. We not only played school dances and sorority parties, but we played in bars and had weekly gigs at popular dance clubs.

The final SRO group that I played with consisted of Dale Taylor, Ed and Greg Sarley, Tom Madej and myself. I was certainly glad that this SRO had a road crew to carry and set up all the heavy equipment because I was now playing a Hammond on stage.

When I first started looking for a job so I could purchase band equipment it was a problem. Being only thirteen years old, I could only work at Bauman's Garden Center. It was licensed as being a farm, so under aged kids were allowed to work there. Even though it was quite a distance from my house, I could still walk to it.

I worked there almost every day after school and on weekends; but I still found time to squeeze in homework, band practice and playing gigs. This routine continued all the way through high school. It was hard but it was worth it. I was doing what I wanted to do. Standing on that stage and playing rock music was an experience beyond words. I felt like a rock star.

Although I needed it to support my newly unfolding rock and roll life, the behind-the-scenes reality of my job was not so glamorous. All my experiences at Bauman's were diverse to say the least. I did everything from potting plants to painting the top of glass greenhouses. This painting job was very precarious because I could only stand on the gutters between the greenhouses. I would place my feet facing in opposite directions while carrying a heavy metal pump sprayer. Slowly I would inch my way across, trying to keep my balance so I didn't fall through the glass and kill myself.

I remember another very hot summer day when I was given a very shitty job to do. I mean that literally. It was shit. I had to dig down, find and unclog a septic tank that was overflowing. The job was dirty and stinky but the money was needed. It was amazing the things I did to be able to play rock music in our band.

My best friend Ed Sarley also worked there for a time. Much to our boss's dismay, we would place different sized plastic pots upside-down directly under the rain drops falling from the greenhouse glass roof. It made a very interesting percussive sound and it drove everyone crazy. It was one of our favorite things to do!

I worked with some other great people at Bauman's like John Banaszak and his brother Nick. John went on to be a three-time Super Bowl Champion playing with the Pittsburg Steelers. I remember John and I having to unload an entire semi-truck, just the two of us. It was stacked full of 6 cubic ft. bags of peat moss. As we got to the center of the truck the heat rose to well over 100 degrees. The intense heat was draining our strength. We had to start dragging the bags instead of carrying them. We persevered, continued on and finally got the job done. The work may have been hard but the money was good, and I was becoming self-sufficient. I was able to buy my own clothes, purchase needed band gear and was even able to afford a car.

It was at Bauman's that I even learned to drive. One day the owner asked me, "Can you drive a truck?"

I really didn't know anything about driving a stick shift, and I didn't have a license, but being a normal teenage boy of fourteen I said, "Yes."

Before long, I was making floral deliveries to various flower shops all over Cleveland in a UPS style step van. I was so proud.

Image 12: **That's Me playing Bass Guitar.**
Ed Sarley taught me.

Image 13: **Just a few guys from our first Standing Room Only band**. Left to right, Alan Chupa, Jim Stamper and Ed Sarley.

Image 14: **Second group of SRO band members**, Rich Reising, me, Steve Knill, Jim Stamper. Top of truck Frank Barrett.

Image 15: **Final SRO band members,** Ed Sarley, Tom Madej, Dale Taylor, Greg Sarley and me.

4

GEORGEISMS

仝仝仝

Working at Bauman's may have been physically tasking, but my four years at St. Ignatius High School were mentally exhausting. The school had special rules for everything. It had mandates about the vast amount of required academic subjects you had to take. It had specific rules on the way you had to do everything including homework. And of course, it had strict regulations about how to dress and a code of conduct that required absolute conformity.

These rules and regulations made it almost impossible to balance work, school and most importantly being a rock musician and playing gigs. But somehow, I managed to fit it all in including being part of the theater group in which I played Bill Sikes in the play *Oliver*.

Let me share a couple of instances where I was able to circumvent some of Ignatius's more annoying rules and regulations. You may find some explanations to be clever while others funny or stupid, but one thing we can agree upon, they are definitely all Georgeisms.

First, let's address conformity. The dress code stated, "Your hair needs to be in a neat and orderly fashion. It cannot touch your ears or collar."

Well, by the time I was about to start my senior year I was playing out two to three nights a week. My hair like any other young rock musician was down to my shoulders. Unfortunately, school was about to start and my options to deal with this problem were limited. I certainly didn't want to piss off any of the Jesuit priests, especially during my senior year. I needed to figure out how I was going to get around this rule, and fast.

One option was I could cut my hair, but that was never going to happen. So, I went with the only option left. I would wear a short hair wig to school. I bought an expensive, natural looking wig that matched my hair color. I put my real hair in a ponytail and pinned it on top of my head. Then, I placed the wig on my head and made sure it didn't touch my ears or collar. I shaved any of my own hair that grew below the back edge of the wig. It looked like my real hair and was a perfect solution.

It must have been pretty convincing, because I wasn't called into the assistant principal's office until a few months into the school year. I walked into Mr. Gramata's office, sat down, and didn't say a word.

He sat forward in his chair and looking at my wig he said, "Mr. Sipl, we need to address this issue."

I cleared my throat and sat up straight in my chair. I pointed to my ears and collar as I respectfully recited back to him the school dress code exactly as written in our school manual, "Your hair needs to be in a neat and orderly fashion. It cannot touch your ears or collar." He sat silent for a moment, and then with a bit of a smile on his face and a nod of his head he said, "Thank you Mr. Sipl, you may go." That's all that was ever said about it. I breathed a huge sigh of relief. I could get through my senior year and still keep my long hair.

At the end of the year I passed the wig on to another long-haired friend named Casey. He needed it for a job interview. Not surprisingly, Ignatius modified the school dress code the following year. It specified "No wigs."

Unbeknownst to me, someone saved that wig. They presented it back to me at our 25th school reunion. It brought back fond memories and really made me smile!

***

Another dumb St. Ignatius rule concerned pens. You could only do your homework using a fountain pen, but while in class you must use a ballpoint pen. Supposedly, this was to keep students from getting their homework done during school hours. Homework at home, schoolwork at school, what a waste of good study hall time.

It seems the teachers could check this by licking their finger and rubbing it across the page. If it smudged, it was ink. If it didn't, it was ballpoint pen and you had to do the assignment over. That was tough, especially when it was a 500-word essay.

Needless to say, there was a way around that stupid rule. We would take a hypodermic needle and insert fountain pen ink into an empty Bic ballpoint pen cartridge. That enabled us to achieve a desired test smear on all homework papers completed during school time.

This alternative worked fine, unless you accidentally put this pen into your shirt pocket upside down. Yes, it would leak! You could always tell which kids had a special homework pen, because they would walk around the whole day with a blue stain running down the front of their shirt. I was lucky. I never had a leaking pen and I was never asked to do an assignment over. My homework always passed the smear test.

Well, how am I doing so far? Are you finding these anecdotes funny, stupid, or most likely, just standard Georgeisms? Anyway, here's the last one I'll share.

***

Ignatius had a demerit system. If you did something wrong, you would get a demerit. After so many demerits you would serve your detention on a Saturday. But it just wasn't sitting in detention as depicted in the classic movie *The Breakfast Club*. Instead, you would have to memorize some Shakespeare soliloquy, or even a presidential speech.

In my four years at Ignatius, I never had to serve a detention. Not that I didn't do anything wrong, I just did all my little witticisms in front of everyone. I used a respectful tone and had a knack for timing. This made the teachers feel that I was not being disruptive or disrespectful. These witticisms were accepted most of the time with a small smile, a little laugh and a quiet, "Thank you Mr. Sipl."

One day before my second-year Latin class started, I wrote on the board, "Beware of Greeks bearing Trojans." When our teacher Mr. Powers walked in, he stopped, read it and then immediately erased it. He never asked who did it. I'm sure he had an idea, but again I dodged the demerit.

***

St. Ignatius was known for their academics and sports, but in the area of creative arts choices were limited. But one beacon of light for the school's creative and talented was the Harlequin club. It was a group that attracted singers, dancers, actors, some directors, musicians and artists.

Being an all-boys school, we would partner with Magnificat, Lourdes Academy and St. Joseph's Academy which were the all-girls Catholic High Schools nearby. Productions consisted of both large musicals and smaller productions. We did *Oliver*, *Fiorello* and *The Man Who Came to Dinner*.

Some of my fondest memories come from the time spent with the talented Harlequin thespians. Casey Batule, Jim Breiner and my best partner in crime, George Buza were among my favorites. How could I not be best friends with someone that has such a cool name as George.

George Buza once told me that the first time he stepped on that stage playing Mr. Bumble in the play *Oliver* he was hooked. He knew that acting was exactly what he wanted to do for the rest of his life. And that is exactly what he did. His career immediately took off and never quit growing.

After graduating from Ignatius, George Buza enrolled in college. After just two weeks of classes, he decided to go to an audition and try out for a part. George was sitting in the waiting room intently going over the lines when the director suddenly appeared. Slowly, the director walked around the room and then stopped right in front of George and said, "Are you here to tryout?"

George was startled and a little confused, thinking, "Why else would I be sitting here studying the script." But being the consummate actor he was, George answered with a serious yet excited tone, "Absolutely, that's exactly what I am here for."

The director grunted a low, "Follow me," and walked through the door.

George Buza quickly grabbed his stuff and followed behind the director, no questions asked. The director had George read for the part. He was instantly hired. George immediately quit college and was on his way to fulfilling his dreams.

When George's contract was up, he was not sure what his next step should be. But he didn't have to worry because the phone rang offering him another acting job, and the rest is history.

George has acted in over 39 major motion pictures, 22 television series and/or animated shows, and is the voice of characters in 4 video games. Currently known for being the voice of The Beast in X-men the Animated Series.

It is always great when I see another creative soul have their dreams come true. The bond of friendship is strong, but the bond that comes from like minds being able to fulfill their creative dreams is timeless.

***

So maybe St. Ignatius did have a small creative side, but for the most part it was known for its academics and being a big football school. Students either fell into the jock category, or fell into the nerd stereotype. I didn't identify with either group. I was somewhere else entirely.

My life was music and rock and roll. You would think that not fitting in would make four years of high school hell. But I was on stage playing two to three times a week in a very popular band, and it was this fact that helped to make my high school life good.

But one negative interaction that experienced still sticks in my mind. Just before graduation the guidance counselor had every senior stop by his office. He asked me, "What do you have planned for your future?"

I told him, "I want to continue playing rock and roll music and eventually become a famous rock star."

With a stunned look on his face, and a very sarcastic tone in his voice, he mumbled, "Well, good luck with that!" He abruptly closed my file, stood up from his desk and said, "Thank you Mr. Sipl, that will be all for today."

Maybe he thought I was just being a smart ass, but I was dead serious. I wish I could show him how wrong he was and how much I have been able to achieve. But he will never know. Unfortunately, he passed away.

***

It was now 1971, and with graduation over, all the confines of high school were finally lifted. I was now eighteen and it was time to move on and go to college. My parents had put aside money for each of their children to attend college. Everything was set to go, or so I thought. When they asked me what my major was going to be, of course I said, "Music." Hearing this, they said they would not pay for college. It was a knife in my heart.

What did they think I would major in? I'd been playing the piano since the age of two. All those years of piano lessons, and never letting me play sports for fear I would hurt my hands. It just didn't make any sense. But they were steadfast. They wouldn't give me a penny unless I became a doctor or lawyer. So, college was now out of the question. Frustrated and angry, I moved out.

Image 16: **I played Bill Sikes** in *Oliver* as a member of the Harlequin club at St. Ignatius.

Image 17: **_Oliver_ Cast**: First row left; I'm the end person with black coat and scarf, and George Buza is front row last person on right with black hat. He played Mr. Bumble.

Image 18A: Above **Jim Breiner (left) and myself (right) in the play *Fiorello*** while at St. Ignatius.

Image 18: Below **George Buza** from X-men series. We were in Harlequin club together at St. Ignatius.

Image 19: Above: **St. Ignatius High School.**

Image 20: Below: **My graduation, 1971.**

5

DEVASTATING REALITY

仝仝仝

I moved in with my then girlfriend Nancy, who lived with her sister in their family home. I was playing gigs with SRO and working at Bauman's, but that just wasn't going to cut it. I now needed to generate more income. I got a job at a plastics fabrication company on the west side of Cleveland. I would be operating a Vacuform molding machine and a hydraulic trim cutting machine. Now I might even have a little extra money to afford tickets to a concert.

It was now the 19th of November, 1971, and it was going to be a great day. I was so excited because I had concert tickets to hear this great new rock group called Yes.

I had only been at my new job for a few months and this was just another typical day, repetitive, noisy and busy. I was focused on creating plastic molds for retail toy packaging. I was using the Vacuform machine. I would then cut them to size using the hydraulic trim cutter.

Hydraulic trim cutters utilized a hydraulic mechanism to cut off the excess plastic around the edge of the mold, using highly sharpened steel blades.

I had just placed a mold into the hydraulic trim cutter. I had my left-hand hovering over the start button and my right hand was adjusting the mold so it lined up perfectly. Just then my boss said something to me. I slightly turned my head to focus on what she said and in that second, I had pushed the start button with my hand still in the machine.

The owner of the company had disconnected the safety so that the machine would not stop as often and run more efficiently. But this also meant it didn't stop if it felt any resistance like a hand still in the machine. As you can imagine, the series of events that were unfolding that day were the perfect setup for a catastrophic outcome and that is exactly what happened.

I pulled my hand out of the machine, the three middle fingers of my right hand had been severed completely through, and were just hanging there attached by small slivers of skin. My boss was screaming, and the owner of the company heard her screams and came running out of his office. Everyone was panicking, blood was gushing out of my hand like a horror movie, but I stayed calm.

I had someone get me a towel. I folded my three hanging fingers into the palm of my hand and made a fist, and wrapped the towel around it to catch any blood. Then, I had them give me a second towel so I could wrap it around my arm and make a tourniquet. Using a piece of wood to twist it, I would tighten and loosen it to allow blood flow. The hospital was not far away, so the owner drove me to the Emergency Room.

The hospital wouldn't treat me until my parents signed forms allowing treatment. I was 18 years old, living on my own, with a draft card offering me a free trip to Nam, but I still had to wait. So, until my parents showed up, the hospital gave me a basin to bleed into and they continued administering the tourniquet.

Presently, my parents arrived and so did the doctor. Even being in a state of trauma, I distinctly remember how my doctor looked. He was noisily chewing gum, and he was dressed in a loud plaid sports coat with a button-down white shirt. He had on white pants, with a white patent leather belt and wore white patent leather shoes. Dr. Radkowski was definitely a character, but he was a top-notch surgeon.

After looking at my hand, he gave me two options. First, he could take off the remaining part of the three fingers to just below the second joint. This would leave me with only fingers stubs, but it was the safest way to go.

The second option was trying to sew everything back together in the hope of saving the fingers, but this would be dangerous. If there wasn't a good blood flow, gangrene could set in, and then I would lose everything down to the palm of my hand, leaving only a thumb and pinky.

Without hesitation, I said, "You have to try to sew them back on, my whole life is music and I play the piano."

Hesitantly, the doctor agreed to try. But just think about it, this was before micro surgery, so the prospects of success were not too high.

After losing so much blood, my body finally gave in and I passed out. The next thing I remember was waking up after surgery. My fingers had been sewn back onto my hand. My hand and wrist were a huge ball of gauze and bandages. The tops of my fingers were sticking out and each finger had a long metal pin protruding from the tip. Each pin was topped with a test tube cork so I wouldn't scratch my face.

It was a devastating reality. I tried not to think negative thoughts about the operation not being a success, but it was hard. I worked at staying positive and was resolute about just moving forward and doing what needed to be done. I reordered my priorities. I was going to focus on healing, making my hand and fingers stronger and more flexible, and then I could get back to my music and playing gigs.

Upon my release from the hospital, I moved back with my girlfriend Nancy and within the year we were married. She was a stable force in this crazy reality I now found myself in. Caring and encouraging, she helped me to navigate it all.

Rehabilitation took a while. I diligently did the exercises to improve strength and mobility. Taking the corks off I even worked at playing the piano before the metal pins were pulled out. Years later when I finally got rid of that piano, you could still see the scratches that were made by the metal pins.

I couldn't wait to get the pins pulled. But as I always say, be careful what you wish for. It was actually the most painful part of the whole devastating ordeal.

I went to see Dr. Radkowski and he thought that things were going very well, so much so that he could now pull the pins out. I smiled, because I was so excited to get them out.

He looked at me with a strange look on his face and said, "You might want to turn your head for this." I watched him pick up a pair of pliers. Yup, everyday household type pliers. He grabbed my hand, held it very tightly and proceeded to pull on the end of one of the pins. OMG, it felt like he was yanking the bone out of my finger. The pliers slipped off of the pin, he grabbed it again and pulled even harder. I passed out.

When I woke up, all the pins had been pulled out. Dr. Radkowski was standing there with a half grin on his face and said, "I warned you to turn your head."

How could I be mad? I was just glad I still had working fingers on my hand that could hurt. Thank you, Dr. Radkowski!

With each passing day my fingers were getting stronger but I was still not ready to return to playing on stage with my band. I had no idea what the future held for me but I knew I had to keep moving forward.

As the year progressed, I worked various short-term jobs just to keep some income flowing. I did everything from washing windows, working on a building site, to working in an office.

***

Working these odd jobs led me to experience some very different life situations that previously were foreign to me. Here are just a couple.

I went to an employment agency. Because I had no college degree and no office experience, they said it would be difficult to find anything for me. As I got up to leave, they asked me if I might be interested in working there. They were spouting that it was an opportunity to make a lot of money in a professional office atmosphere. I should have known better, but as I had nothing to lose I took the job. Of course, it was commission work.

I came in the next day wearing a suit and tie. They gave me a desk and said, "Every morning we start the day with a pep talk from our office manager." Although I had never played team sports, I assumed this was pretty much what happened in a locker room before a game, except we were all in business suits.

And so, my day began. One of the guys took me under his wing and told me what I was expected to do. The job consisted basically of two things, get referrals which entailed cold calling businesses, and interviewing job seekers. I was given a sheet of boilerplate questions to ask the applicant, and that was it. They said I was ready. Really?

Cold calling was awful. After each job applicant's interview, I would immediately have to decide what they were qualified for and start making calls. Since I was new, I got mostly blue-collar applicants to work with. I was calling machine shops. All this did was aggravate the shop owners. They let me know in no uncertain terms that I was disturbing them while they were trying to work. I didn't like any of this and I certainly wasn't good at it. As a matter of fact, in the two weeks I was there I didn't get one job referral.

Then there were the applicants. Just like me, they hadn't gone to college. Some of them had even been fired from their last job. They were just trying to find any kind of work to survive. I really felt for them because before I was sitting on this side of the desk, I was one of them, and I had a feeling that I may be back there soon.

The final blow was an applicant that I had to interview. He was a blue-collar worker. He just wanted a job, ANYTHING! He had a wife and two kids. He cried at my desk, and begged me, "Please Mr. George, I'll take anything! I can't go home with nothing again!"

I held back my tears and told him; I would check the files and call him. I was determined to get this guy a job.

After he left, the office manager came into my office, grabbed the application from my desk and tore it up. He said, "Don't bother with that kind!"

My applicant was black. I was gobsmacked. So, I told the office manager that he was an ass hole for treating anyone in that manner, and I left... For Good!

So again I was unemployed. My father got me a job as a bricklayer's apprentice. The work was at a site in Brunswick, Ohio. We would be building new homes.

My job was basically to supply the bricklayers with blocks or bricks, and to make sure they always had concrete or "mud". The blocks were 16x8x8 inch concrete. They wanted us to carry them four at a time, two blocks in each hand. I thought my fingers were going to rip open. The blocks weighed about 38 pounds apiece, that's 76 pounds I carried in each hand!

Blocks were for the basement; bricks were for the upper exterior. Bricks were carried in a hod. It was a three-sided container with a long handle that you filled with bricks and carried on your shoulder. When the builders got up high, you would have to climb a ladder as you tried to balance the hod full of bricks on your shoulder. It was downright scary.

The concrete was mixed at one location and then dumped into a wheel barrel. We would then take it to where the bricklayer was and shovel the mix onto their palette. If they were up high, they would put two boards down to make a ramp. I would then have to push the wheel barrel up the ramp. Double scary.

The pay was good and I needed the money. So I just persevered and kept working. Back then ten dollars an hour was pretty good for a beginner! Trouble is, it was such hard work that by the time you got home, took a shower and ate dinner, you had no time or energy to spend your money!

This company had a unique and refreshing tradition that I really didn't mind. Every work day around three o'clock, the boss's car could be seen kicking up dust as he drove into the work site. He would have a case of cold beer in the trunk. I've seen feeding time at a farm where the cattle would gather from all corners and that's what this was like. I never liked beer, but working in the hot sun and busting my ass, that beer tasted so good!

We finished the job that summer, but I knew it wasn't for me. Not only was the work really hard but I missed my music and the camaraderie of guys my age. Anybody at the job site who was my age was busy hustling their blocks or concrete to their bricklayers. There was really no time to talk.

I did have conversations with some older bricklayers. But those conversations were mostly about what was on TV, who's screwing whom, and strip joints. None of these were of interest to me. So basically, I just focused on working and not socializing.

It was amazing to think that shortly after my accident I was in a job where I was forced to use the hand that had three fingers sewn back on. But I believe it actually helped with my recovery. It kept my muscles strong and I certainly had good blood flow from the exertion that I put out. It may have been hard but in the long run I benefited from the whole experience.

***

The Office of Workmen's Compensation contacted me. They had decided I was a good candidate for college, and they were going to pay for it. Just think about that: the whole saga of my fingers being cut off began when my parents wouldn't pay for college, and now I was going to go to college because my fingers were cut off. I couldn't pass it up. I attended Cleveland State University, as a Piano major. Ironic, isn't it? I knew I didn't want to end up teaching the High School marching band but I did want to expand my musical knowledge. College turned out to be a beneficial move. The attained knowledge I received was certainly put to good use throughout my lifetime.

Image 21: **Fairview Hospital 1971.** This is where Dr. Radkowski saved my fingers, allowing me to keep my dream of playing rock and roll.

6

I'M BACK

☆☆☆

Finally, Nancy and I moved to our own apartment, where I got the job of custodian. As part of my salary, our apartment on the third floor was free and I got an additional cash stipend on top of that. This gave me some peace of mind regarding income, and it allowed me to focus on getting better, playing my music and attending college. But as always, my first priority was doing my hand exercises, so I could get back to playing on stage.

Custodian work was interesting. There was always something to do, or more likely for me to learn how to do it. One day I was vacuuming the hall rug on the first floor. I noticed a faint odor, a little like sewer gas. I checked the laundry room, nothing. Maybe somebody was cooking cabbage or something. Nobody had complained so I thought that was probably the reason for the odor.

Then, the next week when I was again vacuuming on the first floor the odor was even worse. What was It?

One of the tenants heard me in the hall and asked me if there was anything I could do about it! We walked up and down the hall sniffing doorways. Finally, stopping in front of one apartment we decided it was definitely coming from there.

I looked at the tenant and nervously asked her, "Have you seen old man Adams lately?"

She replied, "No. Come to think of it, his car hasn't moved in the parking lot in a while."

OH SHIT, I screamed in my head, and I felt my heart drop!

Nothing more needed to be said. I got out my passkey and unlocked the door. I couldn't even step in; the odor was that overwhelming. I caught a glimpse of a dark lump in the bed and slammed the door shut and said, "I *think* he's dead!"

Now if you lived in Lakewood in the 60's and 70's, there was a bit of tension between the local officers and the hippies. I had long hair and a beard, so by police standards I would fall into the hippie category.

I called the Lakewood police and told them who I was, and said, "I *think* I found one of my tenants dead." Within a few minutes, a police car rolled up and out stepped my worst nightmare.

This guy was over six feet tall, butch haircut and had a snarl on his face before even talking to me.

Taking off his mirrored sunglasses he barked, "Are you the custodian?"

"Yes sir," I said respectfully.

Tilting his head, he took a step closer and said, "Just what do you mean you *think* he's dead?" as he continued to glare at me.

"Well sir, I guess for sure he's dead." Feeling somewhat intimidated I started to mumble a little.

He scoffed like he didn't believe a word that I was saying. He seemed annoyed and with the wave of his hand he ordered me with his next question, "Well, where is this apartment?"

I took him to the door and unlocked it. He grabbed the knob with his right hand, stepped in and froze. He never took his hand off that door knob, and it was a good thing because he went weak in the knees. He stepped back slammed the door shut and leaned against it. He was absolutely white faced and slumped shouldered and with a shaky voice he said, "He's dead!"

No shit, Sherlock! I thought. Boy, I really enjoyed seeing this macho guy crumble!

Mr. Adams had no family. So, all the neighbors did what we could to remember him in our own way.

***

And so, my life continued. I worked in the apartment complex, did my exercises, practiced my keyboards, and went to school.

Ultimately, all that exercising and determination finally paid off. Even Dr. Radkowski was pleasantly surprised. I really think he was quite proud of his own handy work. No pun intended. I had good circulation, movement and strength. But unfortunately, the tip of each finger had no feeling and I could not make a fist because the top joint of each finger would not bend. This may have been an impediment to some, especially a keyboard player. But as always, I just got creative and worked around it. I had to adjust my finger pressure and the angle I used to strike the keys, but I was able to make the adjustments and effortlessly play the piano.

At long last, after a year of dedication and resolve the big night came. I was able to stand on stage and play a gig with my band, SRO. I cannot explain the feeling of excitement, euphoria and outright relief that overcame me being able to play on that stage again. I had done it. I was really back!

***

I had forgotten how interesting playing gigs could be. Our band SRO was now traveling fairly lightly. This allowed for quick set up and tear down and it saved on paying a road crew. We got a gig at a downtown bar called the Round Table. The bar had quite a long history. Built in 1889, it was first called the Casino Restaurant. Then in 1964 It reopened as the Round Table until it finally closed in 1977.

What was so unique about this restaurant was its staircase. It had a hand carved, ornate wooden staircase which, because of its uniqueness and beauty was later moved to The Atrium Restaurant in Westlake. So basically, what I'm saying was that this establishment was a little high class for a rock band, or so I thought.

I was usually the first to show at gigs. I always liked to have my keyboards set up and ready. Then I could help set up the PA while the other guys set up their equipment. The entire setup was nothing elaborate, since everything fit in the trunks of our cars.

It was about forty-five minutes before the gig. I had just finished my set up and was waiting for the rest of the band to arrive.

Suddenly a tall, rather imposing broad- shouldered "gentleman" came up to me and said, "Da boss wants to see you in his office."

Seemed like an offer I couldn't refuse. So, up the winding staircase and down the hall we walked. We arrived at two huge hand carved wooden doors. The very large "gentleman" raised is right hand, made a fist and gave three knocks. And then he just waited. It was surreal. I felt like I was on some kind of a movie set.

Finally, I heard a husky voice say, "Enter."

He pushed the two-doors at once and they flung wide open. What I saw when the doors opened was a massive, beautifully carved wooden desk. Behind the desk was a rather heavy-set balding man dressed in a white shirt with his sleeves rolled up. He had a fat cigar hanging out of the side of his mouth. Flanking him on both sides were two more very large "gentlemen" in suits. Just as big as the guy that escorted me up there, but these guys were just standing there with their arms crossed in front of them.

It was just like in an old black and white detective movie. Not sure if I should be scared or laugh. I picked scared, so I just stood there silently and waited.

The man behind the desk finally looked up and without even taking the cigar out of his mouth said, "You in da band?"

Feeling the need to be polite, I replied, "Yes, sir."

"Where da boys at?" he grunted.

I told him, "They are on their way. We still have forty-five minutes before we start playing."

He took the cigar out of his mouth, leaned forward and put his elbows on the desk and in a gravelly voice questioned, "You gonna start on time?"

I swallowed hard, and said, "Yes, sir!"

His answered me with a quick, "Well, you better make sure of it."

He then sat back in his chair and put the cigar back in his mouth. He never said another word. I was ushered out.

As I came down the stairs, I saw that the other band members had arrived and were setting up. I was never so happy to see them. And yes, we absolutely did start on time. Wouldn't you!

Image 22: **Staircase at The Round Table** Bar and Restaurant.

7

MAGIC

全全全

Yes, I was back, but that only meant that the same routine of work, school, band practice and playing gigs could continue. I was primed for the next step, but I was not sure what that should be, and then it materialized.

It was now 1972 and Steve Knill, from our old SRO band, approached me and asked if I was interested in forming a new band with Dan Hrdlicka, Don Krueger, Rich Reising, Steve Knill and myself. Having played with both Steve and Rich before, I knew it would be a top-notch band with no egos involved. It didn't take much convincing before I said, "Yes."

We were known as Magic. Maybe our name was a foreshadowing of what was to come. I felt this was a key move and an important step to achieving my dream. A dream I thought may never happen after severing my fingers.

Magic was definitely a forward-thinking band. Each member had a unique perspective and an individual talent that collectively formed a fusion of creativity and invention. We molded the band's sound into something that was magical.

I sang vocals and played the Hammond. I loved that I could select harmonics using the drawbars and create a totally new sound. It was a creative extension of my many years of just playing the piano.

Don Krueger played the drums and also sang vocals. He was an exceptionally talented young drummer. Don and I hit it off immediately. We both had a sense of rebellion in us, yet at the same time a willingness to work with others.

Steve Knill sang vocals and was a solid bass player. He played flawlessly on stage. You could always count on Steve being spot on.

Dan Hrdlicka sang vocals, played guitar, and was known for his local hit song, *Stop Wait and Listen* which he wrote while in the band Circus.

Rich Reising also sang vocals and played guitar and keyboards. He was multi-talented and arranged most all of our material. He was the hub around which we all revolved.

Magic was professionally, as well as commercially successful. We didn't have to survive by playing gig to gig and hoping that the next booking would appear. We were on salary and were booked three to four times a week. We played every Wednesday at the Cleveland Agora, every Thursday at the Corral in Olmsted Township, as well as assorted venues throughout Ohio.

***

Once we were playing in Columbus, Ohio and were on the bill with Bob Seger and his Silver Bullet Band. I was standing waiting for soundcheck to begin, when I noticed two members of Bob Seger's Band standing in the wings.

They were snickering and pointing at my keyboard setup. I wasn't quite sure what it was all about but they seemed to be pointing at the Vox Continental I had on top of my Hammond. It was a little off-putting but soundcheck was about to start and I needed to focus on that.

Our performance that night was tight and when we played *Funeral for A Friend*, we received thunderous applause. As I was leaving the stage, Robyn Robins the Keyboardist from Bob Seger's Band came running up to me. Maybe now I was going to find out what he found so funny about my keyboard setup. Instead, he wanted to know exactly how I was able to get those great string sounds out of the Vox. He wasn't laughing now. He was impressed.

Robyn Robins went on to become an acclaimed producer and mastering engineer. He is one of the most sought-after producers and has accrued production credits on over sixty gold and Platinum Albums. So, looking back I take his inquiry as a huge compliment.

***

Magic was known for the unique material we performed. Not many bands played MacArthur Park or Funeral for A Friend. We even used some pyrotechnics. Once when we first started using them, it didn't go as planned. Because of the billowing smoke the place had to be evacuated. It was no surprise, that particular venue never had us back again.

Another part of Magic's acclaim came from our amazing vocal harmonies. Our voices blended in five-part harmony, creating that recognizable California sun-surf sound. We would perform a Beach Boys' medley to vast audience approval.

***

Magic played a number of venues throughout the Northern Ohio area. One place was a club called Big Dick's in Lorain, Ohio. It was a large club, owned by an interesting character known as Big Dick. His ads clearly stated, "Everyone loves Big Dick!"

In those days, bands played from 10:00 P.M. until 2:00 A.M. Even though I was younger, it was still a very long, tiring night. Don't forget, that after the gig we would help the road crew pack up and get on their way. When we were done, we didn't want to hang around. We just wanted to go home.

On one particular night, we finished performing to a good-sized crowd. After packing our gear, we were totally exhausted. We just wanted to get paid and go home. I went into Dick's office and said, "We are all set, if you could pay us, we'll be on our way."

Dick looked at me with a kind of evil glance and said, "No, I feel like drinking tonight. Why don't you guys stay and drink with me!"

I had driven Dan and Don to the gig and knew we were all anxious to leave. I said, "C'mon Dick, we really need to get going!"

He sat back, opened his top drawer, pulled out a revolver and said, "Nah, I think we're drinking tonight!"

I didn't necessarily believe he would use the gun, but he had had a few too many drinks already and I was not ready to test that theory. So, I said, "OK, let's have a few!"

The three of us bellied up to the bar and Dick went behind to bartend. He pulled out a few trays of lemons and limes, a couple of salt shakers and three bottles of tequila! Whoa, this wasn't going to be good, and I was so right!

Shot after shot, Dick kept pouring. He wouldn't pay us until we drank our respective bottles. I don't know if you've ever consumed so much alcohol that it gets to the point where it makes no difference if you drink more. I feel sure that we hit that point!

We finished our bottles, got our money, and were finally on our way home. It took all three of us to drive the car. We stayed on the back roads and took it slow. Not only were we drunk but it was about five in the morning. We were moving targets for the police.

With some help from the Almighty, we made it home! As I stumbled into my garage, I saw an old baseball bat sitting in the corner. I have no idea where that came from as I didn't play any sports, but I grabbed it and began to crawl up the stairs.

My wife, Nancy who heard me coming up the stairs asked me in an already knowing voice, "Are you alright? I could smell the alcohol as you were crawling up the stairs!"

I handed her the bat and said, "Beat me to death, I don't want to see tomorrow!"

I flopped down onto the bed and passed out! When I woke up, I was still seriously drunk! I thought maybe I'd beaten the hangover! No such luck! The next day was when the hangover set in, and it was a doozy! To this day, I can't even smell tequila without feeing nauseous!

***

I remember many years later, I was at a bar with my step son Alan on his 21st birthday. We decided to have a shot to celebrate his coming of age. Alan wanted to get shots of tequila.

I said, "No, I'll have a shot of Jack!"

Alan insisted on tequila and said, "I'll even buy us both a shot of Patron!"

It was his birthday, so I finally gave in and said, "OK, but I warn you. It will probably be a waste of money."

The bartender poured us each a shot of Patron, and gave us some limes and a salt shaker. We made the customary Happy Birthday toast, and down it went!

I gagged a little as I swallowed and sat for a minute hoping everything would stay down. But alas, I quickly had to excuse myself, go into the bathroom and I promptly threw up!

When I returned, Alan had a slight smile on his face, and there sitting on the bar was a shot of Jack waiting for me. It's really was amazing, even after all those years I still couldn't stomach a shot of tequila.

It was an expensive lesson learned, but at least this time Alan was paying for it. Well, I guess I did too!

Image 23A: Above: **It's just me.**

Image 23**B**: Below: **Magic Logo.**

Image 23: **Band Magic;** Dan Hrdlicka, Steve Knill, Rich Reising, Donny Krueger and me.

Image 24: **Donny Krueger,** Drummer from Magic.

Image 25: **Big Dick's Flyer from 1974.**

Image 26: **Band Magic 1974;** Steve Knill, Rich Reising, Donny Krueger, Dan Hrdlicka and me.

Image 27: **Magic Reunion 1985;**
Front: Steve Knill, Donny Krueger, me.
Back: Dan Hrdlicka, Rich Reising,

8
Becoming ECB,
Eric Carmen's Band

仝仝仝

One Christmas night in 1974, Magic was playing at the Cleveland Agora along with the Raspberries. We were in our dressing room practicing our five-part harmonies for the Beach Boys song *Little Saint Nick* when Eric Carmen suddenly walked in. He just stopped in his tracks and listened. It was the first time I had met him, but it wouldn't be the last.

Eric would often come to see us perform. He even brought his manager in from New York to hear us play. It was almost like being auditioned, and it turned out that's just what it was. When Eric's former band The Raspberries broke up, he asked us to be his new band. It was the offer of our dreams, so of course we said, "Yes." We were stoked and ready to go. We had worked hard as a team, and now all five members of Magic would become Eric Carmen's Band.

***

It was now 1975, and we had come a long way since Steve Knill had approached me in 1972 to form Magic. Our dream had now become reality. We were now the Eric Carmen Band.

Eric decided to add a second drummer, Mike McBride. Mike had played with Eric in the Raspberries. So now with our new seven-member band, we went to ODO studio in New York to record the first album. It was a lot of work and it didn't always run smoothly.

Jimmy Ienner our producer was a hard task master, but Jimmy and I always got along. I wasn't afraid of him, I just respected him and I felt he knew it.

One day, Jimmy and I were putting down some Moog synthesizer tracks in the studio. We had to pause because Jimmy had to take a quick meeting with some suit. He was in the control room talking with this guy when I realized he hadn't muted me out. Remembering that I had a program on my synthesizer that sounded like a train coming closer and closer and then passing by, I called it up and pressed the key.

In the control room, the train sound was progressively getting louder and louder. Both Jimmy and the suit were looking around, not knowing where the sound was coming from. In unison, they both locked eyes on me. I was standing there with a sheepish look on my face and my finger holding down the key. To my relief, they both started laughing. I was glad they both thought it was funny.

There is time to work, and time to play, and knowing when to do which is all about the timing.

Reading the vibe in the air that day, I felt that this was the perfect time to send that train through the control room. It seemed by Jimmy's hardy laugh that he also agreed.

Finally, the album was completed. Clive Davis decided our single from the album would be *All by Myself* and to promote the album we were going on tour.

Brian Gary Varga joined the tour as production manager. He knew and could fix anything. With seven musicians, a grand piano, two full drum setups, three guitars, one bass, five electronic keyboards, and an additional percussion setup, he certainly had his hands full.

***

In preparation for the tour, we went to Atlanta and played some test shows at Alex Cooley's Electric Ballroom. We then went on to California to do final rehearsals at A&R Studios. They had full stage setups which allowed bands to practice their full tour show with sound and lighting. A&R definitely was the place to be if you were going on tour.

Dolly Parton was there rehearsing for her tour. I was so impressed by how gracious she was and how she really listened with interest to what you were saying. She couldn't have been nicer. On a side note, I was struck by how petite she really was.

Down the hall David Soul of the T.V. show Starsky & Hutch was also rehearsing with his band. David would come to our stage, drink our beer and listen to us play.

One day all the guys decided they were going out on the town. I was tired and didn't feel like going, so I asked if someone would drive me back to the hotel first. To my surprise David raised his hand and said, "I'll drive you."

So off we went. We walked out to the parking area and there was David's car, a small two door convertible with the top down. And just like in his T.V. show he hopped in behind the steering wheel without even opening the door.

We stopped at a nearby convenience store. David ran in and bought a 6 pack. With the California sun beaming down on us and the radio blasting, we drank beer and talked music as we sped down the highway. It was very surreal, and a very different time when it comes to having open containers in a car. I wouldn't try that now.

Image 28A: **Whoa, Time for a haircut.**

Image 28: Above: **Magic at the Agora in 1974.**
Back: Dan Hrdlicka, Rich Reising
Front: Me, Steve Knill, Donny Krueger.

Image 29: Below: **Cleveland Agora in 1974.** Line waiting to see Magic.

Image 30: Above: **Eric and me at ECB practice in Cleveland.**

Image 31: Below: **Again, at ECB practice in Cleveland.**

Image 32A: Above: **Eric Carmen Band Logo**.
Image 32: Below: **Our First Album as the ECB (Eric Carmen Band)**,
All by Myself was moving up the charts.

9
TOURING

全全全

Rehearsals were now done and it was time to hit the road. It was November of 1975 and we started our tour with the Beach Boys. Everything was now at a new and very different level for us. From recording studios, to worldwide tours that had us traveling to a new city every day. It was going to be a whirlwind.

We would arrive in a city be driven to the hotel to check in, then go directly to the venue to do soundcheck. We would grab a sandwich from the deli tray in the dressing room, get dressed for the show and wait until it was time to perform. Finally, after we were done performing, we went back into our dressing room to change into our street clothes. Then it was back to our hotel room to play cards, drink and sleep, and just being totally honest maybe even meet some adoring female fan. Before long it was 6:00 A.M. and time to put your bag outside your door and again be driven to the airport to get to the next city. This scenario repeated itself over and over again.

I remember getting on a commercial flight one day and sitting next to an elderly gentleman who was obviously on his first flight! I asked him, "Excuse me sir, where is this plane going?" He looked at me like I had two heads.

Unfortunately, this question was a reality of touring. We would move from one venue to another and not really keep track of the city or state we were going to next.

Touring can be hard, lonely, boring or fun. But for me it was all about the adrenaline rush that couldn't be reproduced anywhere else but on that stage in front of those fans. It was worth any hardships I may have experienced; at least that is what I told myself.

But I do regret the strain it put on my marriage and any hardships it may have caused my wife Nancy. Touring can really take a toll on relationships.

On tour it isn't just traveling from city to city and performing on stage. There are also interviews, radio talk shows, T.V. shows, and critics to contend with. One exciting promotion we did was performing on *The Midnight Special* T.V. show with Helen Reddy as the guest host.

It was a big deal at the time, and I think it helped to push our single *All by Myself* up the charts. Wolfman Jack was there and I also got to meet Henry Winkler and Robin Williams who had stopped by to see the show.

***

One of our earliest shows was at the Bottom Line in New York city. Our set list comprised of mostly songs from the album with a few cover tunes. After the show it was really crowded backstage, you could hardly move. But making his way through the crowd was George Benson the renown guitar player.

He kept saying how much he really loved our arrangement of *On Broadway,* which we had recorded a version of on our album. Three years later George Benson had a hit song. What do you think his hit song was? You guessed it, *On Broadway.* It went #7 on Billboard's Hot 100, and #2 on the soul chart! The arrangement sounded very familiar. Coincidence…I think not.

***

If I get one question about touring that is repeatedly asked of me, it is "What was touring with the Beach Boys like?"

Well, to sum it up in one word, it was *unique.* Mostly, the Beach Boys stayed to themselves. Carl Wilson was the exception. He was friendly, helpful and generally an all-around great person.

On the other hand, Dennis Wilson was just the opposite. I remember one of the Beach Boys' Road crew gesturing toward Dennis saying, "Be careful! You don't ever want to go near Dennis, he'll kill you."

It was a warning he didn't need to give. Just looking at Dennis I don't think anyone would feel comfortable approaching him. I often saw him backstage pacing back and forth like a caged animal. I later found out that Dennis was a friend of Charles Manson. A very scary dude!

I wasn't surprised when one of their road crew mentioned that "There's always a backup drummer available, just in case." But Dennis never missed a show while playing with us.

On a brighter side, touring with the Beach Boys had us performing in huge venues with massive crowds. We were really lucky to be able to perform with them. Not many bands who are touring for the first time get to play with such a critically acclaimed band as the Beach Boys.

Another great aspect of being billed with them is that their music and our music appealed to the same kind of audience. This was unlike some later tours where we were paired up with some hard rock bands. That always made for an interesting evening!

***

One appetizing realization I made while on tour with the Beach Boys was that West Coast tastes in food were way different than mine, or so I thought. I always ate the pastrami and the corned beef deli sandwiches that we would get while recording in New York. Now on tour with these California boys, I was presented with this very unusual looking healthy food. It was the first time, this Westside Cleveland boy had ever tasted an avocado, Swiss cheese, bean sprout sandwich on whole wheat bread. When I first saw it sitting on that tray, I didn't think I would like it. But I was so hungry I ate it anyway. I was so very wrong. It was absolutely delicious and I still eat them to this day.

***

One of the most profound and rewarding experiences I had during the tour was on November 24, 1975 when we played a Beach Boys/Dave Mason concert at the Cleveland Coliseum in Ohio. The dynamics of that event were magical and unexpected. Even though my stage clothes didn't show up, and I had to wear my own street clothes on stage, I was stoked. After all, it was our hometown crowd.

That evening, every action produced a noted reaction. From the anticipation I felt before performing, to the exuberant reaction of the crowd when we walked on stage, to having the crowd sing along to most every song that we played, it was an experience I will never forget. Everything came together that night, I felt that I had finally made it. I was successful, and I was able to give evidence to that in front of my family and friends. It was an affirmation that I had made the right career choice, and not even the severing of my three fingers could keep me down.

The feeling of achievement was profound. But my inner self still realized that every day in every way, I was still just that understated kid from Cleveland, and I was fine with that!

***

I guess being understated isn't a bad thing, unless it almost holds up an entire performance. The day before our Cleveland hometown gig, we were at River Front Stadium in Cincinnati doing another Beach Boys /Dave Mason concert.

Venue personnel asked us to move our band vehicles so that the Beach Boys could pull their limo through the huge equipment door. Our road crew was busy getting last minute adjustments done before we went on stage. To help out, Don Krueger our drummer and myself volunteered to move the vehicles.

We dutifully moved them to the back of the parking lot and returned to the door where we came out.

Unfortunately, it was now closed and locked. We started banging on the door but got no response.

The only alternative was to walk around the front of the stadium and enter through those doors. When we got to the front, we had to cut in line to talk to the girl in the ticket booth. We showed her our all-access passes, and told her our dilemma.

She looked straight at me and said, "Those passes aren't any good here, you can't go in."

I told her, "If we didn't get in soon, there wouldn't be a show. We were in the opening band and the show can't start if we are not there. You need to let us in!" I guess I was too understated, and didn't look or act the part of a rock musician because she still didn't believe me.

I was getting angry. Raising my voice so that everyone could hear I bellowed, "You need to call security and right now!"

That did it. She called security and immediately they came running out shouting, "Where have you been? Everyone has been looking for you!"

I turned, gave the ticket girl a small chilly smile, and quickly followed behind the security guard. Thankfully, we made it, with not much time to spare.

***

When the Beach Boys tour ended, we continued to tour throughout the United States with other high-profile bands. For months now, we had been touring with some legendary bands, and our single, *All by Myself* was climbing the Billboard chart. You might say, I was living my dream. But was I? I wondered if there indeed was a next step, and what and when would it materialize. Only time would tell.

In February of 1976 we started touring with the band Sweet. The pairing of Eric Carmen with Sweet was unusual to say the least. They were a British glam rock band, and we were definitely not. Their music and our music didn't necessarily appeal to the same audience. Many a night it was a crap shoot when trying to gauge how the audience might respond.

The record company also had us billed with bands like Artful Dodger, Brownsville Station, Kansas, and also with America. Some parings were great, others not so much, but I must say it was always a learning experience.

Touring certainly created diverse memories and some of them were very funny. At least some of us thought they were. To understand our mindset, you need to realize that during any free time the tendency was to drink heavily and get into some kind of creative activity. This usually meant getting into trouble.

The episode I'm sharing happened when we were playing in Florida. I'm not sure even Eric knew who the culprits were.

A group of us, which I remember being Donny, Mike (our sound guy), Mark and myself, were walking through the parking lot after tasting some of the local tavern's spirits. Suddenly, we spotted Eric's rental car. It was parked very close to one of those aluminum storage sheds which wasn't bolted down. What a perfect opportunity, we couldn't pass it up.

So, we diligently walked off the length of the car, and then the shed. After all, we wanted to make sure the car would fit without scratching it. Then in unison, we lifted the shed and placed it over his car.

We took a minute to admire our handy work, and then we just continued on our way, as if this was just a normal occurrence. Nothing was ever mentioned, but I'm sure Eric must have had an idea who did it.

***

Yes, we absolutely did have our fun times, but touring also had its nightmare moments. In New York I learned about playing union venues and how strict they can be. It was almost a total disaster.

During soundcheck I walked behind my keyboards on stage to see if my upper right-hand keyboard was where I needed it to be. Unfortunately, it was a bit askew. So, I moved it, just a little to get it where I needed it.

OMG, the union stage hands threw a fit and nearly walked out! They actually threatened to cancel the whole show because I was doing their job. It was a serious and time-consuming ordeal that took a lot of Midwest soothing and pleading to resolve.

Finally, putting on my most humble face, I had to apologize to the head union guy that came to mediate. I explained to him that I was just a small-town Midwest boy who really didn't understand! Thank goodness, they must have taken pity on me because the show did go on. What an exasperating experience.

So, I can truthfully say that for me touring was a unique learning experience in many different ways. It had its highs and it had its lows. But most of all I learned that it was a slice of life that was not real. It gives a false sense of reality that should not be fully embraced. Real-world interactions and relationships do not and should not work that way.

Image 33A: Above: **Just me before the** *Midnight Special* T.V. show, and a haircut.

Image 35: Above: **On stage during *The Midnight Special* T.V. show.**

Image 36: Below: **In makeup for *Midnight Special* after my haircut.**

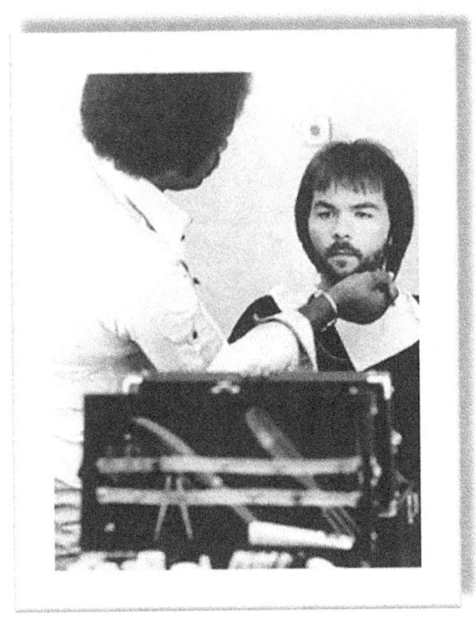

Image 33: Above: *The Midnight Special* T.V. show with Helen Reddy and Wolfman Jack.

Image 34: Below: **Wolfman Jack.**

Image 37: Above: **ECB on stage during *Midnight Special* T.V. show.**

Image 38: Below: **Donny Krueger on drums**, ECB.

Image 39: Above: **Eric Carmen, Me (top right) and Mike McBride (bottom right),** ECB (Eric Carmen's Band).

Image 40: Below: **On stage singing and playing piano** with the ECB, McBride on drums.

Image 41: **Flyer from when we were on tour with the Beach Boys and we played The Cleveland Coliseum.**

Image 42**: On stage at The Cleveland Coliseum** with Eric Carmen on the right. It was our hometown crowd. It was a great night!

Images 43 and 44: Left and Right: **Flyers from when we were on tour with America.** Check out those ticket prices.

Image 45: **My first Gold Record for *All by Myself*. My first million records sold.**

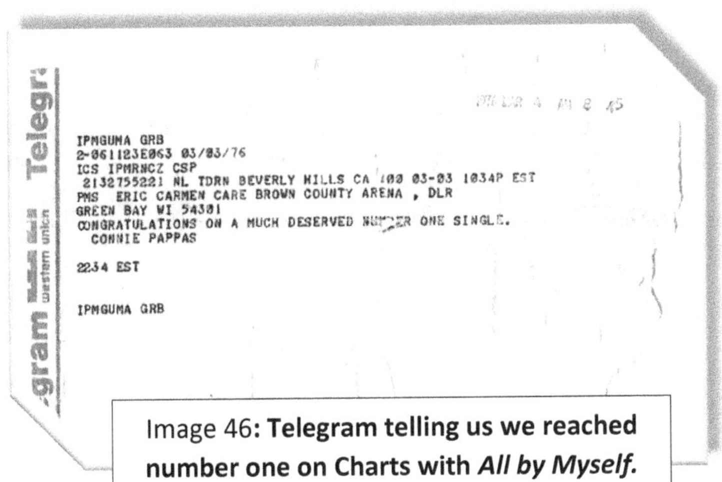

IPMGUMA GRB
2-061123E063 03/03/76
ICS IPMRNCZ CSP
 2132755221 NL TDRN BEVERLY HILLS CA 100 03-03 1034P EST
PMS ERIC CARMEN CARE BROWN COUNTY ARENA , DLR
GREEN BAY WI 54301
CONGRATULATIONS ON A MUCH DESERVED NUMBER ONE SINGLE.
  CONNIE PAPPAS

2234 EST

IPMGUMA GRB

Image 46: **Telegram telling us we reached number one on Charts with *All by Myself.***

Image 47: Below: **Our schedule from when we toured with Sweet.**
New city or state almost every day.

RE: SWEET TOUR
ERIC CARMEN

January 19 & 20 - Rehearsal - Memorial Aud. Chattanooga,Tenn.

Jan. 21 - Memorial Aud. Chattanooga,Tenn. - Phil Lashinskyan.

Jan. 22 - War Memorial.Aud. Nashville,Tenn. - Joe Sullivan & Steve Greil

Jan. 23 - Hulman Civic Univ. Center, Terre Haute,Ind. Phil Lashinsky

Jan. 24 - OPEN

Jan. 28 - Vets Memorial, Columbus,Ohio - Dave Lucas

Jan. 29 - Convention Center, Indianapolis,Ind. - Bob Young

Jan. 30 - Aragon, Chicago,Ill. Jerry Mickelson -

Jan. 31 - Music Hall, Cleveland,Ohio - Jules Belkin

February 1 - Civic Center, Charleston,W.Va. - Phil Lashinsky

Feb. 5 - OPEN

Feb. 6 - Orpheum Theatre, Boston,Mass. - Don Law

Feb. 7 - Century Theatre, Buffalo, NY - Harvey Weinstein:

Feb. 8 - Massey Hall, Toronto,Canada - Martin Onrot-

Feb. 11 - OPEN

Feb. 12 - Stanley Theatre, Pittsburgh,Pa. - Richard Engler

Feb. 13 - Tower Theatre, Philadelphia,Pa. - Larry Magidc-

Feb. 14 - Constitution Hall, Washington, DC - Jack Boyle

Feb. 15 - Mosque, Richmond,Va. - Phil Lashinsky

Feb. 18 - Music Hall, Memphis, Tenn. - Bob Kelly

Feb. 19 - Fox Theatre, Atlanta, Ga. - Alex Cooley

Image 48: **RCA Flyer for Sweet.**
The glam rock band that we toured with.

Image 49: **Concert flyer from when we toured with Sweet.**

Image 50: **Image from an article that appeared in the *Scene Magazine*.**

10
THE SECOND ALBUM

仝仝仝

Finally, the tour promoting the first album was over. *All By Myself* had risen to #1 on both Cashbox and Record World charts, and climbed to #2 on the Billboard chart, whereas the album only peaked at #21. So now, it was time to head back home to work on Eric's next album.

But from my perspective the end of the tour was the beginning of the end of our former band playing, recording and touring with Eric as a unit. The vibe in the air was heavy and subdued, and slowly one-by-one people left.

When we got home after the tour, we lost the first two band members. Both Dan Hrdlicka, one of our guitarists, and Steve Knill, our bass player left the band.

There are many reasons why bands break up. From complex personalities, different life circumstances, to musical differences or even different visions of what needs to be accomplished. All of these can be factors in a band dissolving. But in this book, I will not go into the why or why nots. As I said before, I will only share events that took place. I am not a psychologist, so I can only attest to my own mindset on any specific event as I remember it from my point of view. Drawing conclusions, I'll leave to the reader.

With Steve Knill now gone we needed to find someone else to play bass. Luckily, along came Pete Hewlett. He was a young guitar player with an out of this world voice. He could hit high notes that we could only dream of hitting. Pete went on to work with Elton John, Carly Simon and Amy Grant just to name a few. He also sang and toured with Billy Joel, earning him gold and platinum albums as well as an Emmy Award.

Since Pete was usually a guitar player and not a bass player, it meant his fingers would not be primed with the usual bass player calluses. Musically Pete was able to play the bass with ease. Unfortunately, it made his fingers bleed until he was able to build up some callus protection on his fingers. But being the trooper that he was, he never complained. He did everything that was asked of him and he did it well. To this day, Pete is a good friend and I feel blessed to know him.

***

Eric had already written all the new songs for the album so we were now on our way to England to record them. Our new band consisted of Donny Krueger, Mike McBride, Pete Hewlett, Rich Reising, and myself. We recorded at Marquee Studio in Soho. It was originally a small garage studio used by Alex Murray, the Moody Blues manager/producer. It quickly grew in popularity, and was used by the Beatles and Elton John among others. The studio is located down an alley behind the Marquee Club where almost every major English rock band has played.

With the studio and club being so close together we would frequent the club whenever we had a chance.

When I first walked into the club I was in awe and in shock at the same time. The club was a bit seedy but the walls were lined with picture after picture of bands like the Rolling Stones, Led Zeppelin, Jimi Hendrix and the Who, just to name a few. As I continued walking toward the bar, I turned and saw the stage. I was astonished at how tiny it was. How could any band possibly fit on it? Yet every major English rock band had played there.

I continued on to the bar and sat down. The waiter who was long haired, unshaven and dressed rather shabbily walked over to me, leaned on the bar and with a thick English accent asked, "What'll ya 'ave mate?"

I answered, "Scotch and water."

He reared up, looked me straight in the eyes and said, "Don't you Americans ever say please?"

I felt terrible and even embarrassed. I apologized and repeated my request, this time with the word please included. That scenario reminded me to never forget to include my manners in every situation, no matter the circumstances. You are never too old or too young to learn a lesson.

***

The club and studio were not exactly elegant but they both blended perfectly with the rest of the neighborhood in London's West End. They were places where bands felt they could launch their careers and they are both a part of Rock and Roll history.

On the other hand, our accommodations were the total opposite of where we were working. We stayed in a picturesque English town called Henley-on-Thames. The mansion was right out of the movies. It was huge, stately and the river Thames ran right behind it. There was a housekeeper and a limousine with a driver at our beckon call. They really treated us like rock stars. Even so this Westside Boy still did a lot of the cooking.

Speaking of cooking, I had a real learning experience the first night we were in England. Or should I say "Trial by fire?" The whole band went to an Indian restaurant upon our arrival.

The waiter asked me if I like my food hot and of course I said, "Yes, the hotter the better."

Well, that was a big mistake. Curry in England is definitely not the same as back in the United States. I was so very hungry from our long day of travel, that when the curry dish finally arrived, I picked up my fork, scooped up a huge mouthful and just shoved it in my mouth without thinking. Immediately my eyes got wide, my tongue burned and I almost passed out. It actually took my breath away. But it had a good flavor and I didn't want to admit to the rest of the guys that my insides were on fire. So, I just continued eating. Soon I couldn't even feel my tongue anymore. I was profusely sweating and my eyes were watering, but I didn't give up. I ate, smiled and finished it. We then went back to the house and I died. It's the last time I'll ever do that again. Hot Indian curry is off my menu... FOREVER!

Maybe that's why I cooked so much while staying in the Mansion. It kept me safe from any more menu debacles.

Because the mansion was devoid of food, I went grocery shopping for everyone. I remember pulling up to the store in the limo and having people point and stare. That was awkward but fun at the same time. Of course, the bill was always huge, which in turn would generate an abundance of value stamps. They are much like the old Top Value or S&H Green Stamps in the U.S. that could be redeemed for merchandise. Since I didn't need them, I asked the woman behind me if she saved them. Her eyes got big and she said, "Oh my dear, yes." I gave them to her and she practically cried for joy! I really enjoyed that!

***

The mansion was beautiful and enjoyable to live in, but the thrill of being in the studio was epic. The first time I walked into the Marquee Studio, Elton John had just left and nothing had been torn down.

Gus Dudgeon, who was Elton John's producer and now ours, had miked Elton's piano in a unique way. There was a box built across the whole top of the piano strings, and only a cut out to allow mikes to be placed inside. I was drawn to it like a magnet. Soon people got busy and I was left alone. Naturally, I took the opportunity to sit down and play the keys that Elton had just been playing. It was a special moment that I will never forget.

But as fate would have it, when I played Elton's piano it would be the only time, I got to play anything. I did not play a single note on Eric's second album. When recording, the first tracks that are laid down are the basic tracks, which include drums, bass, guitar and/or piano. My synthesizer tracks would be recorded later, and that never happened. I never had a chance to lay down any tracks.

Gus Dudgeon our producer, just wasn't satisfied with anything that was being recorded. Gus even brought in some studio musicians to play, but that didn't please him either.

Band members started disappearing back to the United States. First Donny Krueger left, then Mike McBride. I was really upset when Donny left to go home. He had been a good friend and roommate since the very beginning. He was and still is a gifted drummer. After all these years, I am still proud to call him my friend.

Before too long everyone was gone. I was also sent home but was kept on retainer. Eric, Gus and Rich went to California to record the album, but that didn't work out as expected. Gus got mad and just walked out, leaving Eric to finish the album by himself, which he did.

So, it was now the Spring of 1977 and I was back in Ohio on retainer. This meant the management company paid me so I didn't join another band and would be available when they needed me for the tour. Sounds like a good deal and it can be, as long as the management company keeps their end of the contract.

In readiness for our next tour all the synthesizers that I used on the road had come home with me. At first, things ran smoothly, but then the checks stopped coming. I had a wife, house payments and needed some consistent income and that was not happening.

I contacted the management company and asked if I was no longer on retainer. They assured me I was, and that the money was in the mail. When that didn't happen, I sent them an official letter stating that I would be selling their synthesizers to recoup the money they owed me. I received no reply, so I started to sell the equipment.

I kept detailed records of what I sold, how much I sold it for, and who bought it. It was now a matter of principle.

Finally, when all was said and done, the management company assessed the transaction records I kept, paid the rest of the money they owed me and replaced the synthesizers that were sold. I then went on tour with Eric to promote his second album. It all worked out in the end, but I still feel that management companies consistently use and abuse their hired musicians and road crews. All we are to them are hired help, and that's exactly how they treated us.

It was now October of 1977, and I was on the road again. This time we were touring to promote Eric's second album, *Boats Against the Current* which he ended up producing himself. Rich and I were the only members from the old band that went on tour with Eric. I also remember that Richie Zito played lead guitar with us while on tour. Richie later became an acclaimed producer winning Producer of The Year in 1990.

We were touring with Hall and Oates. Our first concert was at The Aladdin Theatre in the Aladdin Hotel in Las Vegas. It was really awesome to see the huge sign out front with 5' letters advertising the concert. But even with all the glitz and glam of Vegas it was not a fulfilling feeling. I knew music held much more for me than what I was doing now. I just needed to keep working, learning, and broadening my skills.

It wasn't long before the record company canceled the tour and Rich and I were back home working on our next project.

Image 51: **Eric Carmen and myself on stage during the Hall and Oates Tour**.
Charcoal sketch by Janet Sipl.

Image 52: **Pete Hewlett**

Image 53: Above: **Eric Carmen album *Boats Against the Current*.** We toured with Hall and Oates to promote the album.

Image 54: Below: **Mansion we stayed at in England** while recording *Boats Against the Current* album.

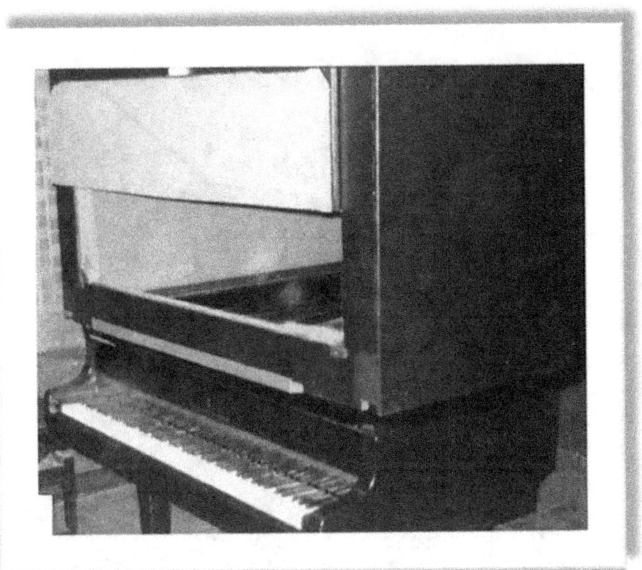

Image 55: Above: **Elton John's piano that I played at Marquee Studio.** It had a unique box built on top of it that Gus Dudgeon used when recording Elton.

Image 56: Below: **Eric Carmen and Gus Dudgeon** while recording *Boats Against the Current*.

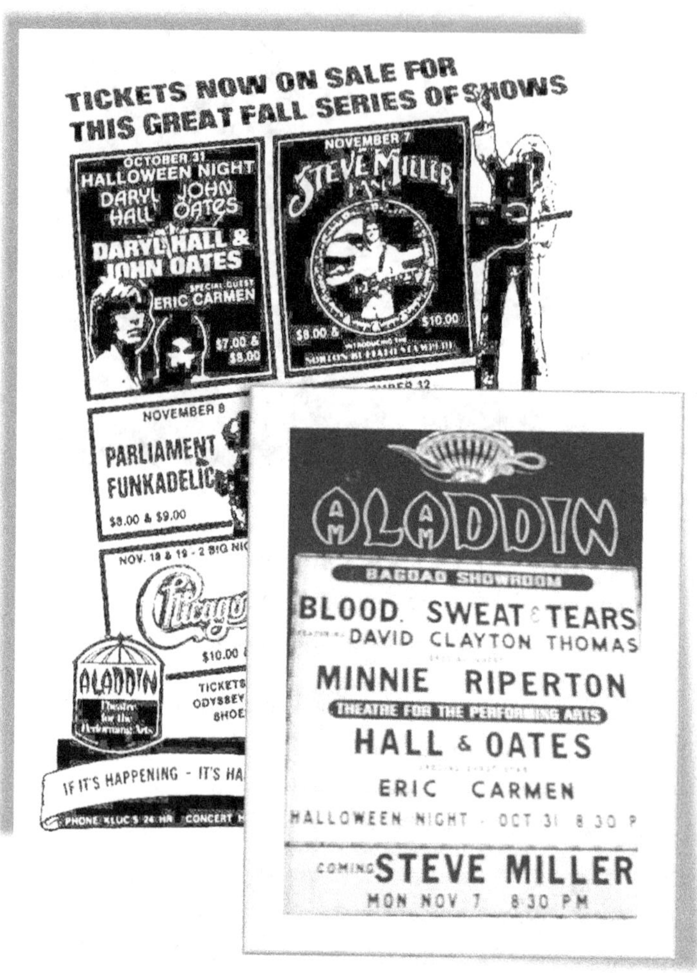

Image 57: Above left: **Flyer for Halloween night at the Aladdin** while on tour with Hall and Oates.

Image 58: Above Right: **Our name on the Marquee Sign at the Aladdin in Las Vegas** during the Hall and Oates Tour.

Image 59: Below left: **Flyer from the final tour date that was cancelled**.

Image 60: Below right: **Stage Manager's note on Cancellation.**

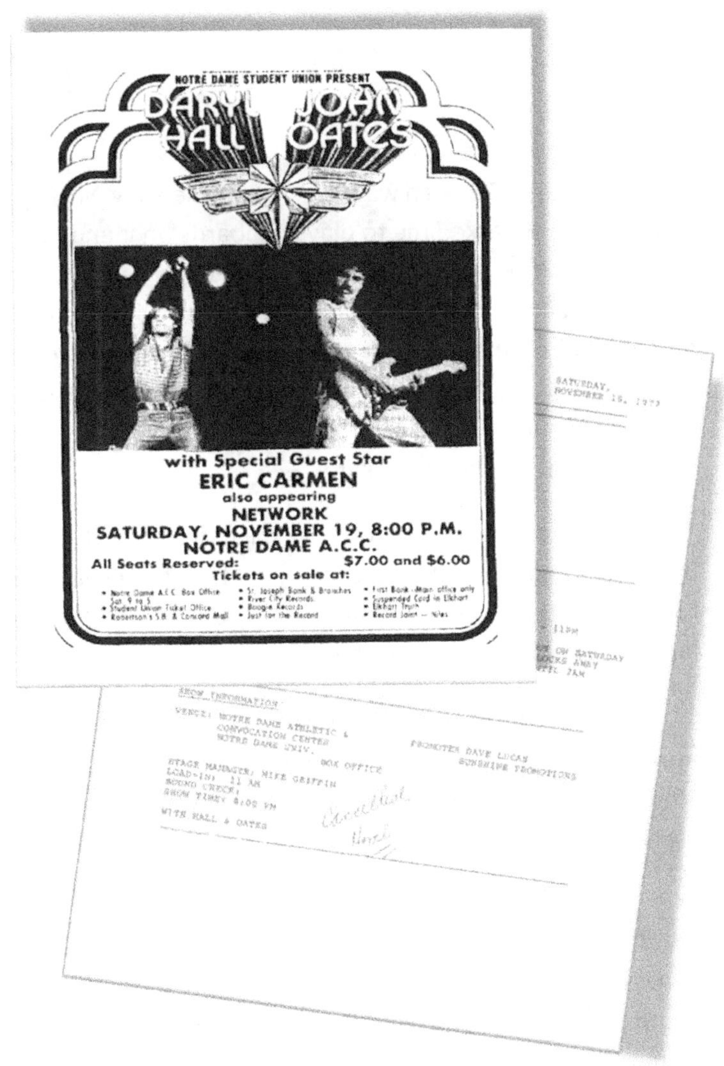

11
WHAT'S NEXT

仝仝仝

It was 1978. Rich was working on the song *No Surf in Cleveland*. He asked me to play keyboards on it and of course I did. It was a worthy cause. All the proceeds would go to the Red Cross. Don Krueger and Pete Hewlett also laid down tracks on the demo. It was the same group of friends again playing together. We were called The Euclid Beach Band. The song was a local hit but it didn't seem to be stimulating any national acclaim.

In the meantime, I was approached by the band Breathless and asked if I wanted to join. I checked with Rich to see if anything was happening with the band and asked him what he thought about the offer.

He said, "Nothing is going on in the foreseeable future so go ahead and join Breathless," which I did. It was 1979, and I signed my contract with Belkin Productions and was now a member of Breathless.

I had my first official practice as a member of Breathless that very week. Rodney Psyka, their percussionist walked up to me and said, "What do you think about Rich and Pete going to New York to record the album?"

I was gobsmacked. Obviously Rich did have something going, he just didn't tell me. All in all, I guess I wasn't surprised. It was just another day in the world of a rock musician.

In the long run it was these types of negative situations that would force me to generate a new path to achieve my goal. You don't get anywhere crying in your beer or staying stagnant at a dead end. Instead, I would learn something new, or apply what I already knew in a different way, and then of course I would continue moving forward.

Implementing new paths and moving forward has always allowed me to be who I am and do what I do. So, thinking about it now, maybe I should just thank all those who were dishonest with me and let me down, or decided to leave me out. They allowed me to go in new and better directions.

Anyway, getting back to Breathless, they were a dynamic, high-energy band. They had all the elements that make a band successful. I was thrilled to be playing with them but my life circumstances called for a change. I had just gotten a divorce and was trying to stay on the straight and narrow. So unfortunately, I needed to leave the band. I actually had to pay Belkin Productions back for the money they invested in me to get out of my contract.

***

I was on my own and I now needed a job. I went to see Kirk Yano, who owned After Dark Recording Studio. Unfortunately, or rather fortunately, he didn't have any studio musician jobs available, but he did need a receptionist. I jumped at the chance. My daily job would be to schedule sessions, do billing and even make coffee, but the best part of this job was accessibility. If someone needed a studio musician, I was handy and could easily step in. But even more than that, I could sit in and work with the engineers and learn.

This apprenticeship sparked my innermost drive to absorb everything I could about audio engineering. It was the right fit and blend of music and creativity. Most bands that came in to the studio didn't have producers, so I did double duty by engineering and producing. This gave me the ability to control and shape the music. I enjoyed every minute of it. While acting in this dual role I got to meet some great people. To this day I am still friends with the band members from the band Northern Lights. Charlie, Doug, John, Scott and Rick, you all still rock!

***

After Dark Studio was growing and doing quite well. Kirk decided to throw a Christmas party and invite our clients and friends. He put no restrictions on who could come as long as they helped with the alcohol supply.

At the time, I was friends with a guy name Tim. He reminded me of a New Jersey thug and even spoke with that "How yous guys doin" accent. Even though he was a little rough around the edges, Tim was an ok guy and we got along.

When Tim heard there was a Christmas party, he asked me if he could come along. I wasn't quite sure how to answer him. The mix of Tim and some of my clients might become awkward. Because it was my place of work, I wanted to avoid any sort of confrontation.

I told him, "I guess it's ok, but you need to understand, there will be a lot of my clients at the party, and maybe some people you might not be accustomed to hanging out with. So, will you be OK with that?"

Tim was like, "Hey, you don't gotta worry 'bout me, I know how ta behave!"

The night of the party was great. Tim and I hung out mostly in the lobby to greet the people coming in. There were even some people I didn't know, so we all introduced ourselves and became buds for the night. Tim was really doing quite well with everyone and I was glad. Most of my uneasiness began to evaporate. I started to relax and have a good time.

Then in walked one of my more flamboyant clients. He announced himself with a loud, "HELLO EVERYONE!"

He saw me and sashayed up to both Tim and myself. I thought, "This oughta be interesting!"

I said, "Hello," and got a hug from Hollywood. I turned to Tim and said, "Tim, this is my friend Hollywood. Hollywood, this is Tim."

Tim cordially shook Hollywood's hand and said, "How ya doin?" Then with a big smile said, "Hey, What's your real name?"

"My name is Hollywood." came the quick reply.

A little agitated Tim repeated "No, I mean like your real name."

Hollywood stood his ground and said, "It is Hollywood!"

To which Tim replied, "I mean, what's your fucking mother call you?"

Even Hollywood had to laugh at that one. It broke the ice and the evening went on uneventfully. I'm glad Tim came to the party.

***

During this time, Craig Balzer from the band American Noise approached me to work on a demo. It needed some embellishing. I laid down some synthesizer tracks and gave the songs a little more punch. It was just what they were looking for, and I was asked to join the band!

Craig sent the demo out to everyone at the national level. American Noise, then known as 747, was not interested in being a local band. The group, which included brothers Craig and Bruce Balzer, Gerry Moran, Greg Holt, Tommy Rich and myself had our eyes set on national recognition. The demo worked. An L.A. manager signed the band and we were on our way. But a manager isn't enough. The band still needed a record deal.

It was 1979 and once again, the wheels were turning on that road to stardom, or so I hoped. I had to try one more time. I think performing on stage never really gets out of your system. It must be worth all the bullshit, because I was willing to repeat it all again.

Al Schlesinger, our L.A. manager had us fly to L.A., California and set up on a rehearsal stage. It was full gear, lighting and sound as if we were putting on a concert. Executives from different record companies came in and watched our show. We repeated that setlist many times that day, with new executives rotating in and out. To our delight, it worked. We were signed to Planet Records and our new name was American Noise.

We then went to Rumbo Recorders to record. It was The Captain & Tennille's brand-new recording studio in Canoga Park, California. Gary Ladinsky, who had worked with Cheap Trick, REO Speedwagon, Quincy Jones, and the Eagles among others, was our producer. It was a good fit and went well. To paraphrase Allmusic.com, the *American Noise* album is "considered to be something of a classic, with the song *Running Through the Night* earning particular praise." We felt we had a good chance of making it big.

But Planet Records was just a new recording company at that time. The only big act they had was the Pointer Sisters. All the promotion money seemed to go to them. We now had this fantastic album, but we didn't get any assistance from Planet Records except they had us make a video. So while still in L.A., we made the video. We were not even sure why, because at the time there was no MTV, so we had no idea what they wanted it for.

***

While American Noise was in Los Angeles, we got invited to some parties and actually had some of our own! I remember one party. It had people jammed in everywhere. There was loud music playing, a lot of drinking and everyone was having a great time.

I understood the beer was located in the fridge in the kitchen so off I went. I was alone, digging through the variety of beers in the fridge when a rather tall man with long hair and a very bushy moustache drooping way over his lips walked in. I looked up. He held up his two fingers holding a good-sized joint in them. He nodded his head as he held up the doob and I nodded in response. We sat down at the kitchen table, fired it up and passed it back and forth. Although we never said a word there was a familiarity to this guy. I knew I had seen him somewhere before!

So as not to ruin the moment, we sat in silence and got a good buzz on. When we finished, he stood up nodded his head again and walked out. I sat there for a moment getting my shit together and trying to recall where I'd seen this person before. Then it hit me like a ton of bricks. That was Jeff "Skunk" Baxter. If you don't know the name, he was one of the founding members of Steely Dan. And at the time of this encounter, he was a member of the Doobie Brothers.

I was extremely impressed by him as a musician. He was one of the early users of guitar synthesizers in rock music. His musical work continues on today with solo albums and session work.

But even more impressive, later in life he actually worked with the Pentagon's Missile Defense Agency and became a consultant to the US Department of Defense! So, I guess smoking that doob didn't hurt any of his brain cells!

To think, I split a doob with one of the Doobie Brothers!

***

When we were finally done recording, making videos and having parties in L.A., we flew back to Ohio. But we still were only playing locally. Planet Records did not pay for a tour, which record companies normally do when a band puts out a new album. We did play out occasionally doing concerts as the headliner but only in Ohio. We also did some radio shows as promotion. WMMS, our local Rock station gave us a lot of air play and we were winning a lot of acclaim, but it wasn't the national recognition we needed. It was such a disappointment.

Obviously, very little money was coming in. I was back to living in a small apartment in Lakewood, upstairs from Educator's Music Annex. I had to sell my house in the divorce. My car died and my sister gave me $1000 to buy a used Mustang. But I needed to work to continue eating and living.

Since Craig Balzer, Tommy Rich and I were in the band together we got a job with a landscaping company. Oddly enough, the owner was Primo Bonfanti, the brother of the Raspberries drummer Jim Bonfanti.

Our job was to get the dump truck in the morning that was loaded with mowers and edgers, then go cut the lawns at Apartment complexes and condominiums where Primo had contracts.

Because Craig got us the job (and was the lead singer) he drove the sit-down mower. Tommy and I took the motorized edgers. That meant 8 hours of the strap digging into your shoulder while your arms scream in pain from the redundant motion.

When done we would load up the truck, drive back to the storage area, fill the gas tanks and clean the mowers. This meant scraping wet grass and dog shit from the bottom of the mower. I'm glad this job was only for the summer.

Hard to believe that three years ago, I was touring with Eric and the Beach Boys!

Twenty years later, I happened to meet a former executive from Planet Record's parent company, Warner Elektra. He said he remembered the band and made a point of saying, "Boy, our company really dropped the ball with you guys." Yup, you sure did!

Of all the bands I worked with American Noise had the most potential to become an epic rock band. We played all our own material, had a group of young good-looking guys and conveyed the energy that was needed on stage. Our sound was unique and notable. It was not just a copy of the usual mainstream rock. The songs had a hook and received critical acclaim, but we were never exposed to a national audience. The group continued to write new material and record but nothing ever came of all the dedication, energy and talent. So yes, the record company really did drop the ball and they dropped us!

***

I want to make it clear that although the record company did not support us, our local radio stations did. They promoted us, played our record, and even had us in for interviews. They did everything they could to help us.

To this day, there are still people out there supporting and helping local and national unknowns. The biggest name in Cleveland that does this is Ray Carr, who won the Cleveland Music Award for Best Radio Show Host.

The Ray Carr Show features in-depth, live interviews with prominent movers-and-shakers and Hollywood A-Listers. It plays unusual oldies and comedy interludes from the 1950s, '60s and early 70's. It features eclectic, rare and amazing music rarely heard on radio. Thank you, Ray. Cleveland is lucky to have you.

***

Just a quick fun trivia fact about the band is that American Noise's album cover made an appearance in the movie *Pretty in Pink*, when a customer shopping in Trax Records picked our album up while browsing. Check it out.

***

Even during those hectic couple of years with American Noise, I was still doing sessions at After Dark Recording Studio to make ends meet. Now I was back to working there full time. I was getting a reputation of being a very good engineer and people were asking for me to do their sessions. It was often a 24-hour day with me even having to spend many a night at the studio. I felt since I was bringing people in I should be getting paid more than minimum wage. Kirk kept promising a raise but it never happened. I went looking for some supplemental income freelancing at another studio, or maybe even a higher paying job.

So, on a Saturday in 1982, I went to a new studio in Beachwood, Ohio called The Recording Connection. It was one of a kind for this area. The whole building was built from the ground up by a studio architect. It had multiple studios that were expansive and contained the latest equipment. One studio even had 48 track capabilities. Quite a step up from what I had been using.

I met with the owner Arnie Rosenberg. Having known Arnie before, I gave him a quick overview of my current situation and then asked if he had any sessions that I could work on as the engineer.

He sat forward in his chair and said, "I been hearing about you. You're building quite a reputation as a top-notch engineer." Then he sat back and said, "I have a gospel session tomorrow, are you interested?"

WOW, I didn't see that coming. I hadn't even seen the studio yet. I didn't know the board or even where he kept the microphones, but I said, "Yes!"

Arnie then took me on a tour, showed me where everything was, and let me get familiar with the board. I showed up the next day and did the session. I was nervous, but it ran smoothly and the gospel group was very happy. More importantly, so was Arnie.

I was so excited about my additional new prospects, but I still had my work at After Dark. So off I went on Monday morning, to do my everyday routine at the studio. I walked up to the door and it was locked. Puzzled, I called Kirk to see what was going on and was told I was no longer employed there. He had changed the locks so I couldn't get in. He had found out about my session at The Recording Connection on Sunday, got mad, changed the locks and then without any notice, fired me on Monday.

Immediately, I went to The Recording Connection and told Arnie that I was now available for full-time work if he needed me. I was hired on the spot. What a whirlwind! I go looking for work on a Saturday, have my first session on Sunday, get locked out of my old job on Monday, and end up with a full time, higher paying job in a better studio on the same day.

People say I was lucky but I don't believe in luck. Rather, I feel luck is any individual taking advantage of everyday opportunities that are placed in front of them, and using them to their advantage. It's up to me to create my own future. When I hit a dead end, I don't keep butting my head against a wall. I take a step sideways, learn, make changes and move forward.

This step in my career turned out to be a pivotal one. Not only did it send me forward, working at a higher level in the world of rock'n'roll, but it also opened up new opportunities to use my musical skills and creativity in terms of writing, producing and engineering music. It was going to be a whole new world and I was ready.

Image 61: Above: **I split a doob with one of the Doobie Brothers!**

Image 61A: Above: **Movie *Pretty in Pink.***

Image 61B: Below: **Movie Scene**: *American Noise Album* cover was in the movie *Pretty in Pink.*

Image 62: Above: Photo taken **while I was a member of the Euclid Beach Band.**

Image 63: Below: **When I was in the band Breathless**: Front Row, Jonah Koslen, Rodney Psyka, Back Row, Kevin Valentine, Bob Benjamin, Alan Green and myself.

Image 64: Above: **Again, when I was in Breathless.** Kevin Valentine, Me, Alan Green, Jonah Koslen, Bob Benjamin, Rodney Psyka, Ricky Bell.

Image 65: Below: **While I was recording the band Northern Lights:** Doug McWilliams, Rick Rasgaitis, Charlie DenHeijer, John Millward.

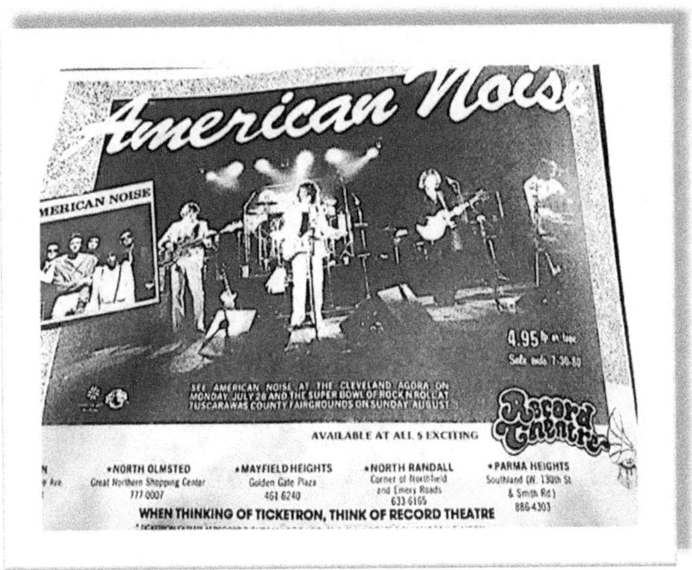

Image 66: Above: **Full page Ad for American Noise.**

Image 67: Below: **American Noise:** Greg Holt, Tommy Rich, Craig Balzer, Me, Bruce Balzer, Gerry Moran

Image 68: Above: **American Noise and friends**. Front Row: Bruce Balzer, Craig Balzer, Me, Tommy Rich, Middle Row: Gerry Moran, Kid Leo, unknow girl, John Gorman, unknown guy, Back Row: Greg Holt, Murray Saul.

Image 69: Below: **Playing keys for the American Noise Video.**

Image 70: Above: **Recording American Noise Album**: I wrote the string charts and conducted the strings.

Image 71: Below: **Zig Zag papers for sale in California vending machine.**

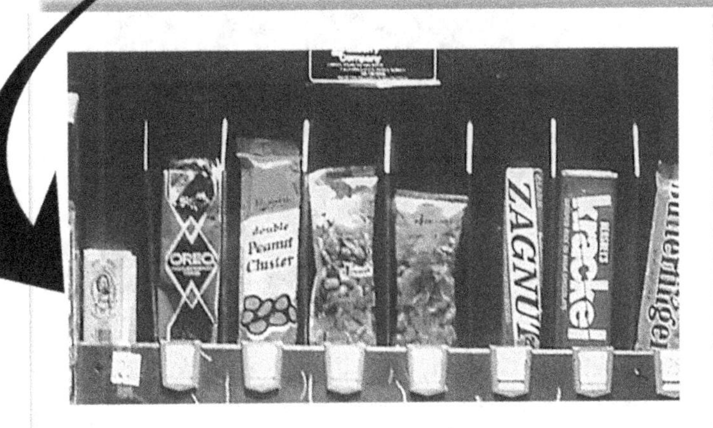

Image 72: Above: ***American Noise Album***: Me, Bruce Balzer, Greg Holt, Tommy Rich, Craig Balzer, Gerry Moran.

Image 73: Below: **Just me, American Noise album photo**.

Image 74: Above: **American Noise**: Me, Greg Holt, Tommy Rich, Craig Balzer, Bruce Balzer, Gerry Moran.

Image 75: **American Noise on stage at the Agora**: Bruce Balzer, Greg Holt, Craig Balzer, and myself.

12
RECORDING CONNECTION

仝仝仝

At the Recording Connection I was able to fine tune my engineering skills. My musical past in rock'n'roll combined with what I learned in college gave me the structured foundation to understand the ins and outs of recording. But more importantly, I was able to polish the skill of knowing what a band wants and what was needed to get there. I certainly wasn't an engineer who just pushed buttons. I had developed the ability to straddle that fine line between offering suggestions and stepping on toes and I used it.

Recording someone's album is a unique and gratifying experience, but it is also very personal. Working with music that is new and fresh and seeing it molded and shaped into an entity unto itself is unique. I not only want technical perfection on my part, but I want the song to reflect the feeling and personal view of the musician. I want the mix to capture and hold the listener so they can't get the song out of their head.

This philosophy seemed to work for me. As my reputation grew, I became more in demand. I mixed Beau Coup's single, *Somewhere Out in The Night*, as well as albums for the bands Fayrewether, Color Me Gone, and Unknown Stranger, formally known as Love Affair.

I was working with Barry Mraz the producer for Unknown Stranger. Barry had also worked with Styx doing production and engineering work so he knew his stuff. With each session I was learning tips and ideas from the best. I would then assimilate these ideas into my own bag of tricks.

Before working with Barry Mraz, I would always use a drum booth to record drums. A drum booth tended to give a dry and sterile sound and we would have to do a lot of mixing to make the drum sound alive. Barry on the other hand, insisted we use the live room to record the drums. It was amazing. The sound was vibrant and alive. Needless to say, I have never used a drum booth since.

***

I also engineered for the band Exotic Birds, recording two of their albums. On the second album, which I recorded a few years later at Beachwood Studios, a new band member was added. It was Trent Reznor who went on to form Nine Inch Nails. Trent was a down to earth, well-mannered individual. We had an excellent working rapport. He was always easy to talk to and was very cooperative when we were recording.

I also ran sound for the band when they did their live performances at the Phantasy Nightclub. Once after a sound check, Andy Kubiszewski their drummer, Trent Reznor, Janet, my soon to be wife and myself were sitting at the bar talking. It was the first time she had met Trent. Later that evening Janet made mention of how kind Trent was and how respectfully he had treated her. To her it was something that really stood out.

Years later after I had married Janet, we were both at home and she was watching MTV. Suddenly, I hear Janet say, "You have got to come and see this, it's Trent and he is wearing a bustier." Whoa, that was surprising but we both chuckled. We never thought of him wearing something like that, let alone for one of his videos. It just wasn't the Trent we knew. On a personal note, it's nice to see him back to how we remembered him before he became famous. He again seems happy and thriving.

***

While at the Recording Connection I didn't just work in the studio. Unlike working at After Dark, Arnie allowed me to freelance. So, I began engineering for the O'Jays. We worked together for over a year. Walt had a studio in his home in Shaker Heights. I would work a couple evening and late nights into the morning, usually from about 8-3AM. I recorded the O'Jays as a group, as well as Levert's demos. He had not as yet become a star and was still just a kid!

I told them I not only engineered but I also played keys. They then asked me to bring my keys for sessions as well. They got a kick out of my "white boy" style as they called it. They'd have me generate and play various ideas. I was surprised and flattered about how many they actually like and ended up using. I felt it was a huge compliment.

As I said, working with them was very interesting. Sessions would start off quite laid back, but as the night went on things got a bit more "recreational." I did stay "non-recreational" so I could keep my brain focused on recording, and we did lay down some dynamite tracks. But no matter, it was always quite the party. They must have trusted me because many times I'd be left in the control room *"All by Myself"*. Come on, you have got to admit that was funny!

I did have one strict policy; I would get paid cash for my work at the end of each night. No cash and I would not return. One evening Walt gave me an "I forgot to go to the bank" scenario and I knew it was over. I assumed they were done with me as they never called again. Hmmm, they still owe me *"Money, Money, Money!"* Now I don't care who you are, you have got to admit this pun was funny!

***

Anyway, the three years that I worked at the Recording Connection were very prosperous and the time just flew by. It was a pleasure to go to work every day. It was great, working with the bands, meeting new people and learning. I loved it!

My whole life has been learning, growing and building a network of people and credentials. In this business it is not just enough to be good at what you do, it is also about who you know, what you have done, and what you can do for them. Getting the job at Recording Connection was a dream come true, but that dream was soon put on hold. The Recording Connection closed and was taken over by EDR, a media company.

EDR Media did mostly corporate media shows with slide presentations, videos, as well as stage productions.

They also did some graphic design and now wanted to add audio recording to the services that they offered. They asked me to stay on and help them make the transition, so I did. This new division of the company was called Beachwood Studios. I was hoping that they would hire me as a manager but instead they hired someone else. Keith was versed in management but had never run a recording studio before. They kept me on as head audio engineer but because Keith didn't have any experience in running a recording studio, I ended up doing all the work of running anything to do with recording. When Keith left, I got his official title because I had been doing the work anyway. Unfortunately, I stayed at my same salary.

Beachwood was starting to grow and there was enough work for another engineer. I happened to be at another recording studio called Britain Square Sound and I met this young engineer who was also a musician. His name was Jim Demain and he really impressed me. He was intelligent, soft spoken, intense and focused all at the same time. He knew his way around the mixing board and had some great ideas. When the session was over I told him if he was ever considering a change there was a job waiting for him at Beachwood.

I was not surprised Jim took me up on the offer. Beachwood was starting to make a name for itself at a national level. Both Jim and I engineered at Beachwood Studios for years. We even collaborated on *Hungry Eyes* for the Dirty Dancing movie, earning us both Platinum Albums 14 times over. Jim went on to be a celebrated mastering engineer, and owns his own company called Yes Master Studio in Nashville.

***

It was at Beachwood Studios that I made my biggest strides toward fulfilling my career goals. Engineering for rock and roll bands had become a major part of my life. I had accumulated engineering, remixing, vocal and performance credits, as well as writing and arranging credits on over 50 albums. But even with all the success, accolades and awards, working at Beachwood Studios was still a roller coaster ride. Over the years Beachwood's daily interactions reflected a company that didn't value its employees. Their one and only focus was the bottom line.

When a negative circumstance would arise, I would focus on what needed to be done so that I could move on. I would find a way to take that negativity and create a positive alternative that would actually allow me to move forward in a purposeful way. Without a doubt working at Beachwood Studios gave me plenty of opportunities to test this personal mindset. A mindset that ultimately determined my happiness and success.

Life at Beachwood was the best of times and it was the worst of times. An apropos saying that perfectly sums up my time there. But on the flip side one of the greatest life changing experiences that has ever happened to me, happened at Beachwood. I met my beautiful wife, Janet. Since she is the one putting my oral life history into book speak format, I know she will be embarrassed about what I am about to say. Without her love, support and encouragement I would not be who I am today. Thank you, and I love you!

Image 76A: Above: **The O'Jays,** Recorded and played keyboards at their home studio.

Image 76: **Recording with Rich Spina, producer Barry Mraz (Styx) and I'm engineering.**

Image 77: Above: **Recording the Exotic Birds,** with me engineering.

Image 78: Below: First *Exotic Birds Album* I recorded.

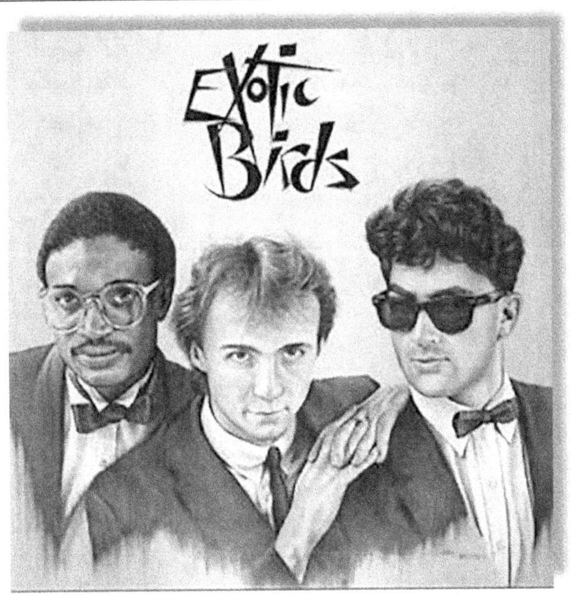

Image 79A: Above: **Exotic Birds with Trent.** Left to right Tom Freer , Trent Renzor, Andy Kubiszewski, Frank Vale, Mark Best.

Image 79: Below: *Exotic Birds Album with Trent Renzor* in the band. I received engineering and producing credits on the album.

13
ONCE UPON A TIME
AT BEACHWOOD

全全全

Meeting my wife Janet was a page out of a storybook. She may have a little different twist to our meeting but this is how I remember it from my point of view. So now, sit back and relax while I tell you our story.

Once upon a time, a beautiful girl was taking a music engineering class at Beachwood Studios. This was surprising since she had absolutely no musical talent whatsoever. But since she had to teach music to her sixth-grade class at St. Peters School, she was looking to the music engineering class to be a solution to her problem.

She was currently working on her masters in computers, so she thought she could incorporate some of the same kind of technical aspects and create a music program that focused on the technical side of music and how music is recorded. She knew she could hook her middle school kids' interest with these kinds of lessons. But more importantly, she wouldn't look like a fool trying to play a piano, a guitar or even trying to sing. Janet wanted to make sure the workshop would present material she could actually use in her classroom. So, it was off to Beachwood she went. And that is how it all began.

The moment I saw her walk in, I immediately felt a connection. Keith Voigt asked me if I had time to take her on a tour. Of course, I said, "Yes."

After I showed her around, we went back to my office to discuss how she might incorporate the information from the workshop into her lessons. It was a comfortable and easy flowing conversation. Time just flew by.

Suddenly I remembered, I had a session scheduled and there was now a band waiting for me in the studio to start a session. When I told her I had a session I think she felt that I was just trying to get rid of her. But that was far from the truth.

Just then Michael Stanley popped his head in and said, "Hey! Don't forget about our session." Janet and I laughed awkwardly and we started to wrap up our chatting. I guess we were longer than I thought because Michael popped his head in again. And like the gentleman he always was, he said with a sly smile, "We're still waiting!"

I quickly walked Janet to the reception area and went to do my session. I was hoping she was going to sign up for the workshop, but I wasn't sure.

When I went into the session, I made an excuse that I needed to get another microphone and I slipped out to quickly make sure that she was signing up for the class. You see, Dale Peters of the James Gang was supposed to teach the class. But now that Janet was in it, I called Dale and told him that he didn't have to teach the class because I was going to teach it.

The classes went by quickly, and at the end of the workshop each student had to do a mix of a band we recorded together and submit it for review. Janet was working alone in the studio when Dale Peters walked in. He stopped and listened to what she was doing, or rather was not doing correctly and stepped in to help. So now Janet had a copy of the mix he helped with, and the one she did by herself. Now, what do you think she did? Yup, she submitted Dale's copy to me for critique.

As soon as I heard it, I knew it couldn't have been her work. On her written critique I wrote, "You must have had an excellent teacher because this mix is far better than anyone would expect from any student in the class."

When she received the critique, she told me what she had done. Then with that cute sly smile of hers she said that she was just testing me to see if I would be critical of her work, just because it was her. I guess I passed that test. She then gave me her own mix. I told her it was a good thing that Dale had helped her with the other mix!

Over the many weeks of the class, we got to know each other well and everything clicked. We had a lot in common, yet we were different in so many ways. We had both been divorced, but she had a teenage son Alan and I had no children. It was the Yin and Yang of relationships, but it worked. We have now been married for over thirty-seven years. Janet was pivotal in getting me through those years at Beachwood and has been there throughout my journey. She is my heart and soul.

***

Meeting Janet was one of the best things to ever happened to me, and it happened at Beachwood Studios. But as I have said before, not everything at Beachwood was positive. I am just happy that Janet was there to help me navigate the rough times.

Looking back at some of the roadblocks I faced at Beachwood, I now see that each one was actually a steppingstone. Each roadblock made me learn something new, do something differently, or even stop what I was doing all together and go in another direction. It was always exciting, but also scary to take that new step.

One of these new direction steps was learning the skill of post-production. This was adding narration, music and special effects to videos. Ultimately this skill led me to writing music for videos, television shows, writing jingles and commercials.

I always felt that with each new step I needed to seamlessly blend the new skill into my current skillset. I never wanted to lose my musical side. It was this ongoing building and blending of skills that allowed me to be happy and successful.

***

As you will see in future chapters, I always stayed true to my musical roots, even when working with corporate clients. I even made time to record rock bands.

One of the bands that I worked with during this time was a band called, 1964. They are a critically acclaimed Beatles tribute band that has traveled all over the world for more than 40 years. *Rolling Stone* called them, "Best Beatles tribute band on earth." They have shared the stage with such diverse bands as Smokey Robinson, The Turtles, Beach Boys, Rod Stewart, as well as AC/DC just to name a few. Their audience appeal is wide spread, as they create their nostalgic magic on stage.

But just looking, sounding and acting exactly like the Beatles is not enough. Each member of 1964 owns the specific period instrument, clothing and wears the hairstyle of the individual Beatles member they are representing. They really make you take a second look as they create the original mania the Beatles had when performing on stage.

Gary Grimes who was the bass player from the band 1964 had a personal commitment to the band that went above and beyond. He was originally a right-handed guitar player. He taught himself to play bass left-handed so he could authentically impersonate Paul McCartney on stage. Everything the band did was accurate to how the Beatles did it, including how I recorded them.

This project took some research and had some unique differences from normal recordings. From the microphone setups, to using only four tracks to record, it was unusual and quite an undertaking. It brought me back to the days when Ed Sarley and I would record in my garage using my father's two track stereo Grundig recorder.

But the coup de gras was the audio compression in the final mix. It was the key to attaining the correct levels to get that specific, authentic Beatles sound. I felt this was important and a bit of history that needed to be preserved. To my great relief, I did it.

Besides recording the band, I ran live sound for them when they were on tour in Montreal, Canada. They would perform in large outdoor venues to huge crowds. Everyone screamed through the whole show. You would think you were at an original Beatles concert. It was a unique experience!

The band, 1964 still tours the world. They have played Carnegie Hall eleven times, performed in the Beatles hometown, and even performed for Heads of State throughout the world. The band members are good friends with George Harrison's sister Louise. John Lennon's wife Yoko Ono has also relayed her heartfelt wishes to them for the band's success.

Gary who lived in Akron, Ohio was a close friend of mine. Unfortunately, he passed away from brain cancer in 2010. That great smile he always shared will be missed. He may be gone but his spirit and music will be forever in our hearts.

***

But rock and roll sessions weren't just for nights and on weekends. They did find a way into my nine to five days, just in a more corporate way. I did monthly rock concerts for the NBC Source Radio Network.

We had a forty-eight-track mobile truck that would go to concert venues and record the concerts live. They would then bring the raw tape back to me in the studio. I would take these raw tracks that had been recorded and set up a rough mix.

Then came the scary part, I would run the tape of the concert from start to finish while doing a live mix. There were no stops and no corrections. It really was a tense situation and if I made a mistake it was broadcast for all to hear. So, I really had to keep my shit together. Some of the concerts I mixed for NBC Radio included the Stray Cats, Golden Earring, Night Ranger and The Pretenders.

I really loved doing my rock sessions, but my call to duty at Beachwood seemed to be doing corporate work. My corporate base was expanding by word of mouth, which in turn added more advertising clients to my daily schedule. But what was special about these advertising sessions is that I was now able to include my music. Again, I was growing. I was able to do more than just record and engineer. My journey was continuing in new and diverse ways without losing the musical side of me.

Image 83: **Michael Stanley.** When I first met Janet at Beachwood Studios, I completely forgot about time. I almost missed my scheduled recording session with Michael and the band.
Charcoal sketch by Janet Sipl.

Image 83: Above: **NBC Source Radio Golden Earring,** concert recording I engineered.

Image 84: Below: **NBC Source Radio Stray Cats,** concert recording I engineered.

Image 85: Above: **NBC Source Radio the Pretenders,** concert recording I engineered.

Image 86: Below: **NBC Source Radio Night Ranger,** concert recording I engineered.

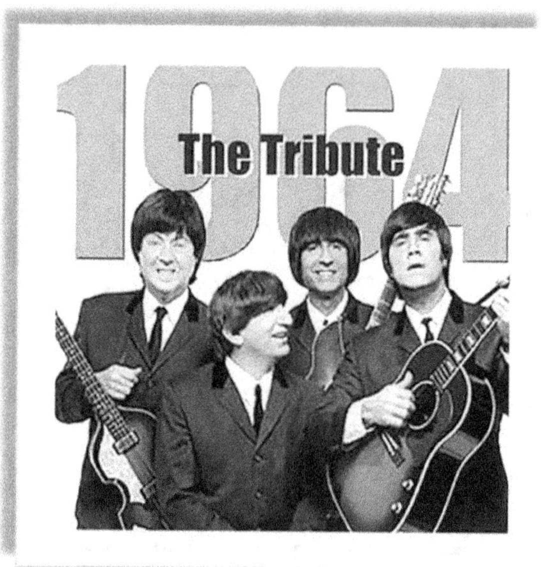

Image 81: Above: **1964 The Tribute Band** that I recorded: Gary Grimes (Paul), Terry Manfredi (Ringo). Tom work (George), Mark Benson (John).

Image 82: Below: **Signed photo of Gary Grimes.** RIP my dear friend.

Image 82A: **Arriving at the Church.**
Our Wedding, 1986.
Image 82B: **My ponytail.** After the wedding, I started growing my hair. It went almost down to my waist.

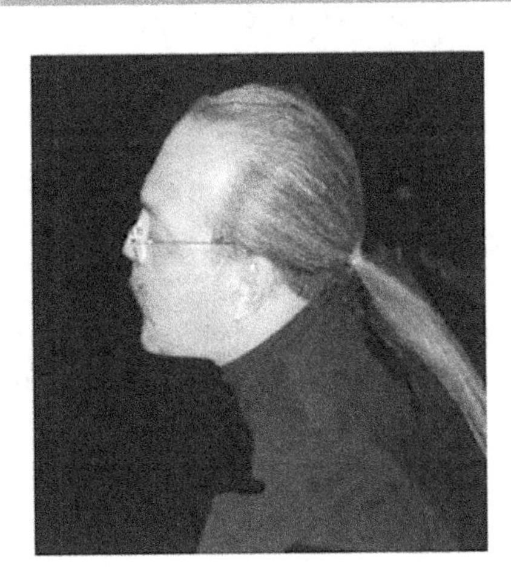

14
ADVERTISING

仝仝仝

When Joel Solloway joined the staff of Beachwood Studios, his expertise was in the area of advertising audio. He had a great corporate client base. He was excellent at closing the corporate deal and I was great at implementing the technical recording side. We created a dynamic team. Things got done, the clients were happy and so was the boss.

It may not be like recording a rock and roll band, but corporate work is not always as dry and boring as you might think. On the contrary, I got to do some interesting projects and work with some very talented people. It also kept me on my toes. I had to create solutions when working with time code, satellite, and phone patches, some of which are still used today as standard format.

Joel was instrumental in adding some fantastic modern technology to our facility. We got a large satellite dish allowing us to do sessions with other cities. But even more importantly, we got a digital recorder and became the first studio in Cleveland to have a tapeless studio. It was a definite game changer.

Using the new equipment, I did a satellite session with Leonard Nimoy and another one with Patrick Stewart. And before you ask; Yes, Leonard Nimoy did tell me to "Live long and prosper" at the end of the session. I reciprocated the greeting and let him know I was giving him the Vulcan salute. It was the best satellite sign-off I have ever had. Both Leonard and Patrick were friendly, funny and very professional all at the same time. They listened and got the job done, but still had time for a little mischief.

***

Clients do a satellite session instead of an in-studio session because it is cheaper than flying a big-name talent to the studio. It's also better for the star because they don't have to stay in a hotel overnight and spend hours on a plane. But one celebrity went against the norm and came into the studio from California. I'm glad he did.

It was toward the end of the work day when we picked up Burgess Meredith at the airport. As befitting a star of his caliber, we picked him up in a stretch limo. Joel and I decided to take Burgess to dinner. Being the wine connoisseur that Burgess was, he ordered a variety of wines before, during and after dinner. Needless to say, we were feeling no pain.

It was getting late so I thought I'd better call my wife and let her know I was still alive and would be home soon. This was before cell phones existed so I used the car phone. I was talking to Janet explaining that I had been out to dinner with Joel and Burgess.

Suddenly Burgess takes the phone and in his best Penguin voice says, "Hey, Janet, Thanks for letting George come with us. The girls think he is a great guy, and we're having a great time in the hot tub."

I quickly took the phone back from him, ready to explain my way out of the situation, but all I heard was my wife laughing. I didn't have to explain. She got it thank goodness.

The next day when Burgess came to the studio to record, he seemed so frail and old and I wondered how on earth he was going to be able to do the job. We sat in the lobby talking and his voice was low and muffled. He didn't sound at all like he did when he played the Penguin in the *Batman* TV series. I gave him the script and we went through it line by line. I was predisposed to the idea that it was not going to be an easy session. He got some tea with honey and we went into the studio to record.

Burgess stepped in front of the microphone, cleared his throat, opened his mouth and blew me away. His voice was clear and gravelly. His cadence and intonation were right out of the movies. There was no doubt that this was the Penguin. He was so precise that he would repeat any line he felt wasn't exactly right. He was a true professional and got the job done.

So just like working with Burgess Meredith or Leonard Nimoy, advertising sessions can be interesting and fun. This made it really nice because they were the bread and butter of Beachwood's income.

***

As I said in the previous chapter, I never wanted to lose the musical side of me. I always tried to incorporate my musical background into my work, and this is how that evolved at Beachwood.

One day Debbie Richards who was one of my advertising clients said, "You play music don't you? Could you write some original music for my video?"

With that one question, a whole new world opened up for me. I was now writing original music for corporate videos, television shows, commercials, and the Cleveland Indians who are now the Cleveland Guardians.

The Cleveland Indians would put out a highlight video at the end of the year to sell to the fans. It was forty-five minutes of original music that had to fit what was going on in the video. What was interesting was that sound effects also had to be added, like a bat hitting a ball, or the sound of a ball hitting the catcher's glove. It was like doing a miniature movie script. Needless to say, it took some time to complete.

I was also writing original music for other Cleveland Indians videos like *A Great New Way to See the Grand Old Game*. I even won an AMI International Festival Award for my music on this video.

It was finally happening. All the diverse skills, talents and interests that I had acquired over the years were coming together and blending into a career that was fulfilling to me. It was very lucrative for Beachwood but not for me. I was still on my original audio engineer's salary even though I was doing so much more.

***

At Beachwood I also did a lot of work with Elaine Rogalski. She was a highly sought-after producer from EDR, our parent company. She created shows for corporate meetings such as Burger King, Sherman Williams, Key Bank and Sunar-Hauserman. These were million-dollar projects and I was writing original music for them.

Elaine wanted to make sure that the music I wrote hit all the key points in the videos. This caused me to have to use varied tempos instead of the standard rock and roll time signature of 4/4 time. I needed to use 5/4 and 7/4 signatures. No pun intended but these were difficult times. Well, maybe it was a pun, but it was still funny.

Anyway, Elaine was a hard task master, but I was able to create what she wanted. I had to rely more on my classical training to compose this type of music, so I'm glad I had the knowledge. I knew those college classes would come in handy one day.

Some of the projects I worked on were created to promote and advanced a positive viewpoint of Cleveland, such as Tower City Center video and the New Cleveland Stadium video. They were rewarding to create and were very successful. All of these projects were focused on helping to erase Cleveland's previous designation of being "The Mistake on The Lake".

***

Even though I worked on these complex projects with high profile clients, my boss still thought of me as "just" that understated, long haired rock musician. Yes, I had a ponytail and it was down to my waist, but I didn't put on any airs. I had regard and consideration for everyone. I treated everyone as a person, not as an object of their success. I was always just me.

My experience with Burger King is a perfect reflection of how I felt. Burger King was a million-dollar project. They had an Indiana Jones theme. We actually built a scaled down replica of Indy's airplane to fit on stage, so that the CEO could walk out of it. During one of our meetings at Burger King's International Headquarters in Florida, Elaine and I were seated next to each other at a long conference table. We were waiting for Burger King's Director of Communications and his entourage to arrive. It was a bit of a wait so we were getting a little anxious.

Finally, the door opened and they walked in. The Communications Director was smiling and walked over to Elaine and said, "Hello, you must be Elaine." They shook hands and exchanged pleasantries. Then he walks up to me, flips up my ponytail and with a big grin on his face said, "And you must be the Creative Director."

I immediately started to laugh and shook his hand firmly. I liked him already. The rest of the day went well. The Communications Director and I really hit it off and it was just Ben and George by the end of the meeting. No formal titles being used.

A month later, the Burger King executives flew into Cleveland. My boss and some other suits from EDR, were standing and talking in the lobby with all their business formality. I walked in and walked straight up to Ben Morse, Burger King's Director of Communications. Everyone went silent and was looking at me, not sure what was happening.

I smiled, put my finger under his tie and flipped it up and said, "Well, you must be the Communications Director."

My boss gasped, and even took a little step back. He stood there with his mouth open, just staring at me.

Ben looked right at me, got the biggest grin on his face and yelled, "George! How have you been?" He put his arms around my shoulders and gave me a big hug. He then patted me on the back, continuing to laugh and exchange quips. My boss didn't know what to make of the exchange. I just think he was glad I hadn't blown a million-dollar deal.

Again, it was me just being me, and the only person who seemed to have a problem with it was my boss. The Burger King's Show was a huge success but it was only part of what I was doing.

I was already writing original music for corporate shows, doing satellite session, as well as voice over sessions and recording bands. Now, I was going to be adding writing jingles to my skillset. Again, my world was expanding.

Image 87: Above: **Joel Solloway**, co-worker from Beachwood Studios.

Image 88A: Above: **Burgess Meredith as the Penguin in *Batman* T.V. series.**

Image 88: Below: **Burgess Meredith and me** at Beachwood Studios.

I recorded both gentlemen while at Beachwood Studios.
Image 89: Above: **Patrick Stewart.**

Image 90: Below: **Leonard Nimoy.** He told me to "Live Long and Prosper" when we were done recording and he gave me his Vulcan salute.

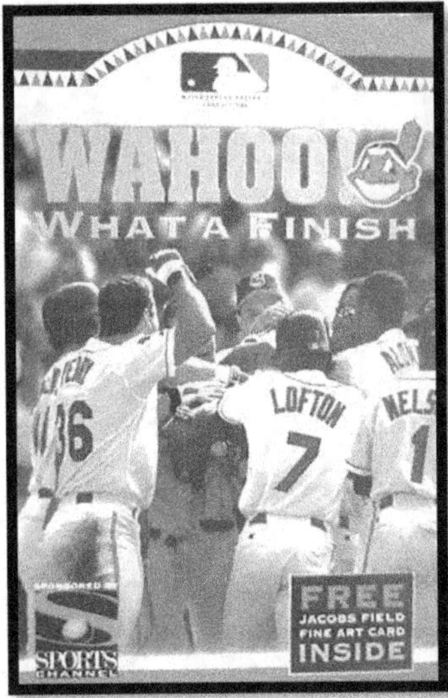

Image 91A:and Image 91 Above: From 1996 through 1999 I did the end of the year **Cleveland Indians VHS video tapes.** I did the assembly, music and sound effects.

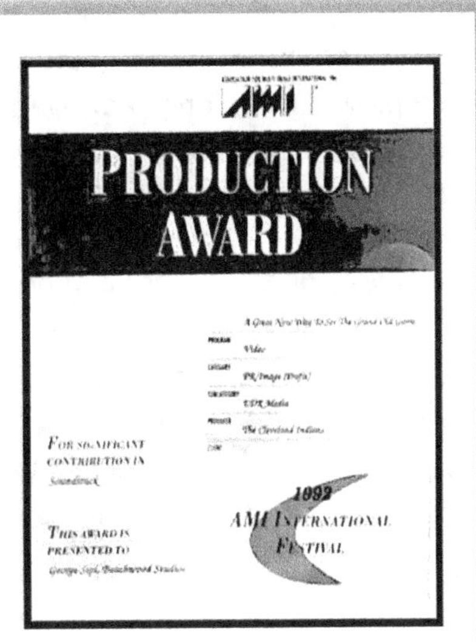

Image 92: **AMI International Festival Award** I received for the soundtrack of the Cleveland Indians 1992 video, A Great New Way to See the Grand Old Game.

15

JINGLES

仝仝仝

I worked with Jim Brickman. Yes, the two-time *Grammy* winner. Back then he was writing jingles and I was his engineer. It was a great learning experience. I attentively watched how he would align the music and words to the client's product. He would create a hook at the beginning which would catch the viewers' attention and make it stick in their mind. Surprisingly, it was the same philosophy I employed when engineering my rock music. It made absolute sense and made my transition into writing jingles fluid. Thank you Jim!

Joel Solloway on the other hand helped with the business side of working with advertising clients. He had a huge client base and was able to establish a positive and productive relationship with them all. He really was a master at his craft. I learned so much from both Jim and Joel and I thank them both for a great start to my Jingle writing career.

***

The first jingle I ever wrote was for a car dealership. It was music with a simple tag line, but it was a lot more involved than just writing the music.

After determining the client's needs and what specific information they wanted in the commercial, I would then have to mold all that information into a cohesive idea keeping in mind the time constraints of a jingle. There is only a limited amount of time so picking the right words to convey their message in a succinct and memorable way was very important.

I would then compose the music and words, making sure that I was hitting all their key points. Writing the music was the easy part, and after working with Elaine Rogalski my key point taskmaster, hitting key points was not a problem either.

Finally, I would play all the instrumental parts I had written as I was recording my own tracks. I would then mix the jingle myself. From start to finish it was a one man show. This was the biggest difference from when I worked with Jim Brickman. He used outside musicians and had me engineer his sessions.

My all-in-one combo platter of skills was great for the client and for Beachwood. They both got a great package deal.

One of my longest running jingles for a car dealership has been running on television since the 1980's. I wrote the music for Spitzer's 85th Anniversary commercial. Even with updated revisions, the original tag line is one that people still sing instead of saying: *Spitzer, Our World Revolves Around You.*

***

There is one area of corporate writing that can sometimes be a problem, and that's the multiple approval levels within a client's organization. Sometimes everyone feels they need to put their two cents in just to justify their position. Ever hear the expression "Too many cooks spoil the broth?"

Here is a prime example. I had a session where the approval hierarchy was not only ridiculous, it was funny. I was recording a commercial for an unnamed company, that had a person talking to a duck. The duck had to respond to what the person was saying. I tried different duck sounds from our library, but the producer just wasn't satisfied on how they sounded when I placed them into the narration. The quacks were lacking inflection, and I agreed. I had tried everything to get a believable duck sound but nothing hit the mark.

Finally, I had an idea. I pushed the record button, ran to the recording booth and started quacking like a duck, as if I was responding to the guy in the narration.

The quacks had inflection and intonation, and when I placed them into the radio spot, it sounded like a real conversation.

The producer from the ad agency was ecstatic. We wrapped the session up and he called his boss to come to the studio to hear the final product. His boss came in, sat down and I played the tape for him.

The producer and I waited in silence. Did he like it or didn't he? He looked up with a serious look on his face and said, "I really like it, but could you make the duck sound more like a male duck?"

We took his suggestion very seriously, until he left the room. Then, we laughed about the whole situation and made absolutely no changes. The ad agency's client absolutely loved the radio spot, especially the talking duck. I guess I must have sounded like a male duck after all.

***

Quacking like a duck was fun, but not at all dangerous. Unlike when I had to create a sound effect for one of my Ohio Lottery commercials, which turned out to be just a little dangerous.

The video for this commercial showed a close-up of a Tachometer and Speedometer on the screen, and as the Lottery jackpot shot up the Tachometer and Speedometer would follow. The motor sounds we had in our sound effects library just didn't work. They just didn't reflect the revving power or timing shown on the video. I needed to create a revving motor sound that I could sync to the action being shown on the screen. So, I brought my Porsche 924 to work so I could record its revving engine.

I put a microphone in the engine and set up a recorder. I had people with walkie-talkies in cars, both in front and behind me. We kept in constant communication.

They were on the lookout for traffic and any police presence. We were on Interstate 271 and I pulled off on the side of the road. When I got their OK, and I was cleared for traffic, I hit the record button and then hit the gas pedal. I took off like a bat out of hell. I hit 110 and that's when I backed off.

It was a success. The recording and final commercial was dynamite, and every time the commercial ran on TV, I remember the thrill of driving my Porsche at 110 mph.

Image 93: **Our screaming red Porsche.** I recorded the engine sound at 110 mph and used it in an Ohio Lottery Commercial.

Image 94: Above: **Jim Brickman-** Worked with Jim Brickman as his engineer on commercials. I learned so much about the business while working with him. Thank you, Jim!

Image 95: **One of the first car Jingles I wrote was the music for *Spitzer, Our World Revolves Around You.***

16
TELEVISION &EMMYS

仝仝仝

For a number of years, I wrote the music for the HGTV series, *Room by Room*. It was a lot of work, but the end product was always rewarding.

Room by Room is still the longest running home decorating show in HGTV history, as it ran for nearly 14 years. It has been shown in over 90 million homes, and it still shows up as reruns to this day.

While working on the show, I not only learned a lot about home repair, but the hosts Matt Fox, Shari Hiller, and I became great friends. Matt lived not too far from me so it made it nice if I ever needed help with some carpentry tips.

Scoring music and adding sound effects to videos and television shows was a fascinating and enlightening experience. It was very much like working on a major motion picture except in miniature.

***

I count myself fortunate to have written the music for three great television documentaries. All three of them won *Emmys* for the music. One of the three, which I actually wrote at my own studio after I had left *Beachwood* was very impactful and really touched me. I can honestly say, this project made me cry. It was called *Finding Aliza*.

The story is about a young Jewish girl who was a Holocaust survivor. Agnes Greenfeld tells her amazing story about when she arrived at Auschwitz concentration camp. After three days of being locked in a cattle car with her family, they arrive at the camp. They pulled her out of line away from her mother, and put her in line with some other young girls.

The Nazis then had these girls strip naked. They lined the girls up, shaved their heads and tattooed a number on their arms. Agnes felt violated and scared. She had a profound sense of loss of self. Her mother, sister, and little brother had been taken to the gas chamber and killed that very day. Why she was not taken she did not know, but she knew she was now alone.

The girls were then marched naked into the showers. Agnes prepared herself for what was coming. Everything she loved was now gone, so she wasn't afraid to die. But standing there alone with no one knowing or caring who she was made her cry. She just wished she could hold someone's hand as she died.

At that moment a girl named Aliza, who was close to Agnes's age and standing by herself, asked Agnes, "Are you alone?"

Agnes answered, "Yes." They clasped each other's hands and gathered strength. They were now ready to endure whatever came next.

It wasn't the gas chamber that day, just an ice-cold shower. Afterwards they were given ill-fitting striped prison garb to wear. They were then marched outside through the mud and filth to their barracks.

When they got to the barracks, Agnes was able to acquire a piece of cloth. She ripped it in half making two triangles. She gave one half to Aliza to use as a headscarf and made one for herself. They were the only two girls in their group able to cover their heads that first day. It was a small act of defiance.

The Nazis wanted to demoralize them by shaving their heads. But Aliza and Agnes decided they would show this seemingly unnoticed act of noncompliance. They wanted all to know that they still held on to self, and would survive.

Throughout all the years in the camp, Agnes and Aliza looked out for one another. They were finally liberated in 1945. The liberation was certainly good news, but the girls were also a little sad. They had become like sisters and now they would be separated.

Both girls went back to their own hometowns, which was the beginning of an almost 50-year separation. Getting married, moving to different countries, and having children made it difficult to reconnect. Agnes spent over 25 years searching for Aliza and finally she found her. What is so touching is that the story is narrated by Agnes herself, and we go on her journey to meet Aliza in real time.

Yes, I cried when I wrote the music, and I absolutely cried again when I watched the documentary. It was a project that really had an impact on me. Maybe it reminded me of my mother, sister, brother and grandmother who were in Gakowa, the forced labor camp during the war.

***

When *Finding Aliza* was nominated for an *Emmy Award*, I was invited to the ceremony. Janet and I dressed in our best and off we went. We were expecting the same theater presentation as the other two *Emmy Award* ceremonies. Well, this one was a little different.

People were sitting at large round tables instead of theater seats. Janet and I opted to take one of the tables in the back, as we were a bit intimidated by the large crowd. We were sitting at a table with people we didn't know. They were busy talking about all the stuff they were involved in and if they would be getting any awards tonight. Janet and I just sat quietly, smiled and listened.

I noticed Michael Stanley was sitting down front with Jan Jones who had the TV show *Cleveland Tonight.* They were a pretty big deal and attracted a lot of attention. I knew and worked with Michael before, but he was busy and it was not the time to walk up and say hello. Although, if I had he would have been fine with it. Remember how Janet and I kept Michael waiting for his session at Beachwood, yet he was still the perfect gentleman?

The time finally came for them to announce the winner of the category in which I had been nominated, *Music Composition for a Documentary Series or Special.*

Whoa, they called my name! Really? Janet had to poke me in the side because I just froze for a minute. I walked up and having no idea what I was going to say. I had not expected to win. I got to the podium and rambled a heartfelt thank you and walked all the way back to our table in stunned amazement. Everyone at the table just stared. I guess they were wondering, Who the hell is this guy? How did he win an *Emmy*?

Now the cool part. From the front table Michael Stanley stood up. Even though the awards show was continuing, everyone was more interested in what Michael was doing! "Is he going for a smoke?" "Is he going to the bathroom?" "Is he sick?" He made his way all the way back to the last table where we were sitting. He came over and shook my hand, patted me on the back and said, "Good to have another rocker as part of this group!" You know, he didn't have to do that! But that was Michael, a real upscale dude. RIP my friend!

***

The personal impact of individual projects was always different. *Finding Aliza* really did take a toll. But now let's look at a different kind of project. I wrote sixteen children's songs for a collection of Richard Scarry's books. It really was fun and uplifting. Every song made me smile or even laugh out loud.

I noticed that all of his books would instantly hook the reader and then kept the reader's interest while they learned about the content presented in the book. So, all the songs I wrote needed to do the same. Again, much like writing a jingle.

And yes, I had to read all the books. And since some of you have asked, "No, the reading level wasn't over my head." Don't tell anyone, but I really enjoyed them.

I made sure each song reflected the theme of the book. I included some of the specific words that Richard Scarry used so there would be continuity between the words of the song and the book.

One of my favorite songs, which was sung by Alex Bevan is called:

Germ Monsters:

The germ monsters live most everywhere,

You can't really see them so please take care

To keep yourself clean from head to toe

Then germ monsters have no place to go

It may not have been a hit rock song, but all the kids at my wife's school loved it. I was the Pied Piper of my whole neighborhood. The whole project was a respite from my usual corporate and rock and roll sessions. It made me feel good.

***

As entertaining and uplifting as the Richard Scarry project was, working on the next project allowed me to be creative in many different ways. I got to work with some of the best people around.

The project entailed working with a lawyer named Jim Berk. We completed three albums together using some of the most talented musicians and singers in the area, including Andy Kubiszewski, Anne Cochran, B.E. Taylor,

Bob Frazier, Donny Iris, Ed Sarley, Gary Grimes, Kevin Raleigh, Pete Hewlett and of course, myself.

The unique aspect of this whole project was that Jim Berk wrote the songs, but he still needed someone to arrange, produce, perform and record them. He felt I was the perfect choice, since I could accommodate all these roles in one package.

Jim wasn't just a lawyer and song writer; he was an idea man. The idea he was promoting was very interesting and innovative for its time. He wanted to create what a web-based application that would allow people to download music for a fee. Sound familiar? Yup, just like ITunes, only ITunes wasn't even thought of yet. He was really ahead of his time. It really was a monumental moneymaking idea, just not for him. Unfortunately, Jim died some years later, and ITunes became a staple in the music business without him. I always thought that maybe his idea for the application came from his desire to just sell his songs.

I sent some of the songs that I recorded with Jim Berk to Jimmy Ienner. Jimmy Ienner and I had first met at ODO Studio in New York back in 1975 when we were working on Eric's first solo album. We always got along and now and then, for this or that, we would be in touch. Whether I like it or not I knew Jimmy would be dead honest with me, and that he was. When he got back to me, he had critiqued the songs. It wasn't good news for Berk. He said the songs had too many words, and the storyline needed to be less complicated. It was just too much.

But one thing he did like was the arrangements and the final mix of the music. He even made mention of some specific things I had incorporated into the mix. Coming from Jimmy Ienner that was a compliment. The last thing he said was, "I always knew you would be the one to make something of yourself." WOW, that was worth a million dollars to me. When someone of that caliber likes how you did something or asks how you got that sound, it is the highest compliment an engineer or producer can get. He made me feel great, actually beyond great. It reminded me of when the keyboard player from Bob Seger's Band asked me how I got those string sounds out of the Vox Continental. It doesn't get any better than that.

***

I don't really know, but maybe that is why Jimmy Ienner called me at Beachwood and asked me to engineer *Hungry Eyes* for the *Dirty Dancing* movie. Jimmy Ienner was now the head of Vestron Pictures and they were putting out the *Dirty Dancing* movie. Unfortunately, I was already committed and working on other projects during the day, so I recommended my protégé Jim Demain to be the engineer. Knowing what a fantastic engineer he was and that it would be beneficial to Jim Demain's career it was a perfect fit all the way around.

So, the recording began. Eric, Jim Demain and Jimmy Ienner got to work laying down tracks. Then Eric and Jim Demain worked on the final mix before sending it to Jimmy Ienner to hear.

I wasn't sure how things went while recording. But the few times that Jimmy Ienner talked to me while at Beachwood he seemed cranky and short. It was just like I had seen him act in New York when things weren't going his way. But since I was busy with my clients and their projects, I didn't get involved.

Some weeks later Jimmy Ienner called me at home and my wife answered the phone. This was long before cell phones or caller ID was able to tell you who was calling. She said, "It's Jimmy Ienner, and I think you'll want to talk to him." She was right.

Jimmy told me that Vestron Pictures and RCA had declined *Hungry Eyes* and would not put it in the movie as is. He said, "They felt it was not finished." Jimmy went on to say, "I want you to go into the studio and do what needs to be done."

So that is exactly what I did. The next day I went into the studio alone and put an old two-inch tape on the machine and transferred all the tracks. I thought I was just creating a demo for Jimmy Ienner to hear. I wanted to see if that's the direction he wanted to go before we got to work. I deleted some tracks, added some new ones, and redid the bells throughout the song. Finally, I sped the whole song up.

Two days later Jimmy flew into Cleveland and came to Beachwood. He walked into the studio and said, "Let's hear what you've done."

I played the tape for him and he said, "That's it, I love it."

WOW, he liked what I did. So, with Jimmy Ienner there to produce and Jim Demain now at my side, I did the final remix, the rest is history. *Hungry Eyes* went to number four on the Billboard chart. Jim Demain and I got platinum albums fourteen times over for remixing it.

I want to thank Jimmy Ienner for calling me and I thank Eric for performing another blockbuster hit. You both are the best!

Image 95A: *Hungry Eyes* **from the Dirty Dancing Movie on a 45.** For all the young people out there, that was a type of record speed and it would also reflect the size of the record.

Image 96A and Image 96: Above: **HGTV Series,**
Room by Room with Matt and Shari. I wrote all the music for
this home improvement series for years. It is the longest
running HGTV home improvement show. It ran for 14 years.

Image 97: Above: ***Emmy* for the soundtrack from *Finding Aliza* Documentary**. One of the three *Emmys* I won for writing a musical score in a documentary.

Image 98: Below: ***Finding Aliza* Documentary, a holocaust story.**

Image 99: Above: **I wrote sixteen children's songs** to go with Richard Scarry's Books. I wrote the Germ Monster song with this book in mind.

Image 100: Below: **Jim Berk and myself in the studio.**

Image 101: Above: **In my office at Beachwood, with my Golden Reel Award for the remix of the song *Hungry Eyes*** from the Dirty Dancing Movie.

Image 102: Below: **Jim Demain and Myself, with our Platinum Records for *Hungry Eyes*,** which went to 14 times Platinum.

Image 103: Above: **Jimmy Ienner, music producer extraordinaire.**

Image 104: Below: ***Dirty Dancing Album*, with *Hungry Eyes* on the soundtrack.**

17

MAKING THE MOVE

☆☆☆

Looking back at the years I had spent at Beachwood and factoring in all the good and bad, I decided my time at Beachwood Studios should be coming to an end. It wasn't just about money, although it could have been. My original music alone was bringing in enough money that it could have been a division unto itself. It was just that in every respect, day in and day out I was feeling unseen and unheard.

Don't get me wrong, it wasn't about seeking verbal acclaim. I was already getting that by way of accumulating National Awards and notoriety. I was respected in my field and had already won two *Emmys,* with a third one coming later. I had also received Gold and Platinum albums for my work. So, receiving acclaim was not the issue.

It was the atmosphere created by management that was the problem. The boss definitely had his favorites, but it was more than that. It was the everyday interactions that made things difficult. They were not positive or beneficial to anyone. To me it was such a simple concept, everyone needs to feel valued and I didn't.

Whenever I would get frustrated and complain about what was going on at work, Janet would ask me, "Why do you need Beachwood? You are the only one writing original music there. All the money that original music generates is because of you." Then she would go on to say, "You know, you can do it on your own." I knew she was right.

It was great to know that she was behind me no matter what. She had a good paying teaching job and we were both covered by her health insurance plan. If I did go on my own having health coverage would take a lot of financial worries off my shoulders. I just needed to get all my ducks in a row before I made a move. I felt that it was coming soon.

I was proud of my roots. I had started as a rock musician and then became an engineer, and now I had added composer to my resume. But to my boss, I was "just" that rock musician. Whoa, there is nothing wrong with being a rock musician, on the contrary! But in his mind that seemed to carry a negative connotation. At least that is the way he made me feel.

A simple example, that perfectly reflects how he made me feel unvalued, was apparent in the scenario surrounding our company's yearly Christmas Wish List. Not that it made a difference to my boss, but I did share this revelation with him. Here is how it all went down.

When I handed in my resignation my boss tried to get me to stay. He was offering all kinds of perks but I said, "It's too late." He wanted to know, what I was talking about.

I asked him, "Do you have the Christmas Wish List that I had filled out this year."

He scoffed and replied, "Of course," as he pulled it from a file drawer.

I then asked, "Did you look at my list?"

Defensively, he started to spout how he always reads them, so he knows what everyone needs, and he starts to read some of the items I had written on my list.

The few things I had listed were items that I could use in the studio. They would make my job easier but more importantly more efficient. They weren't even expensive.

I then asked, "Do you have my lists from past years?"

I knew he would because he keeps everything on file. When he pulled them out, I told him to take a closer look. Glancing at the lists he looked a little perplexed and then he just shut up. All the lists were photocopies. Yes, that's right, they were all exactly the same. I had turned in a photocopy of my Wish List form for the last three years. He hadn't even noticed. My dear boss had been generous with others fulfilling needs from their lists, but I hadn't gotten one single item from mine for the last three years. It was definitely time to go.

When people found out I was going, I don't think that anyone was shocked. But I was shocked that many people were quite negative. I think friends may just have been scared for me while others were just mocking my future plans.

No matter their reasoning I kept hearing the same story over and over again, "Nobody works from home," or "A studio at home will never work," I was even told, "A recording studio at home is not professional, and clients won't come." Well, I was just going to have to prove them all wrong.

To make the transition financially easier I took an interim job at Classic Video in Broadview Heights. My job at Classic was the same as at Beachwood but their equipment and way of doing things was very different. It was a difficult situation, but as always, I knew I had to adapt. Having this job gave me the time I needed to get everything in order for my own business. I knew I could do it!

Janet and I were in the process of building our new home in Olmsted Falls, which really made it a bad time for me to be quitting my job and trying to set up my own business. But that was my situation and I just had to deal with it.

I had to wait until the house was finished before I could complete my studio. I was praying that everything wouldn't take too long. I had taken out a loan in addition to my mortgage so I could build the studio with proper soundproofing and enough space to work and record. I also needed keyboards, microphones, cables, external plugins and a soundboard. Since it was a digital studio, I didn't need a two-inch tape machine. Thank goodness! But I did need recording software, monitors and a computer.

I knew I would not be recording rock bands at home, so the studio size took that into account. For most of my clients, I would be writing original music that I would play and record myself. I would also be doing voice overs and assemblies. All of which involved just me in the studio, no clients or other musicians.

It wasn't long before my home was complete and so was my digital studio. I knew that all my former clients would follow me from Beachwood, so now I was ready to start my new venture in my very own studio. I was now officially George A. Sipl Productions. It was a thrill but still scary.

***

Not only was my new home a great house to build my studio in but it was a fantastic party house. I remember my 40th birthday party. We had over 40 people show up and we literally partied all night. Janet and I learned a long time ago that when we were having a party invite everyone in the neighborhood. That way no one complains because everyone is at the party. The party started at 7:00 p.m. We set up a beer bar downstairs. On the main floor we had a wine bar and a full liquor bar. But the best bar, which was set up on the kitchen island was our specialty coffee bar. It consisted of different mixing stations where we had recipes printed for different kinds of coffee drinks. Each station had all the liquor needed to make that drink. Drinks like Irish Coffee, Keoke Coffee or a Hot White Russian were enjoyed. One thing you can always count on, we never have a party without a coffee bar. It is always a big hit.

Anyway, the party was on a Saturday so a lot of my friends played gigs that night. But no problem, because they all showed up after their gigs. Janet was out front talking with the people in the smoking area. Suddenly, she sees our living room couch being carried out the front door into the garage.

Without batting an eye, she says, "Excuse me gentleman where are you going with my couch?"

Shrugging their shoulders, they answered, "We just needed more room to set up the band."

With a sweet smile on her face, she says, "Well, just put everything back when you are done." Everyone agreed, the band set up and started to play.

It was 3:00 in the morning. The police were driving past the house and they stopped. Their comment to Janet was, "Isn't it a little late to have a band playing, and be so loud?"

She politely asked, "Did someone complain?"

They answered, "No."

To which Janet replied, "I didn't think so, because the whole neighborhood is in the house." We only had 28 homes in our neighborhood.

The two policemen smiled and said," Well, just keep it down." I guess it didn't hurt that she had had one of the policeman's kids in school. All was well the rest of the night, no one ever complained.

Janet went to bed around 6:00 a.m. and said, "Last one out please lock up."

I went to bed shortly after her and yes, the last person out did lock up when they left.

The party was great, but Janet's gift to me was even better. She had a special bass guitar made by Greg Sarley who is Ed Sarley's brother. Greg has worked on some specialized guitars for some well-known artists such as Vince Gil. It was a special gift and I really loved it, but I love her even more. She is a keeper for sure.

Image 105: Above: **First Video Teleconference** with Me, Andy Adamovich, Ed Neal and in back Denny Martin

Image 106: Below: **Working the board at Beachwood Studios.** Charcoal sketch by Janet Sipl.

Image 107: Above: **Behind the board at Beachwood Studios.**

Image 108: Below: **Beachwood Studios**, in Beachwood Ohio. The satellite dish out front was so big the city made us move it.

18

IT WILL NEVER WORK

仝仝仝

It was now 1993, and my brand-spanking-new digital studio was up, running and ready for business. It paralleled the storyline from the 1989 movie *Field of Dreams* when Kevin Costner hears a voice saying "If you build it, they will come." Then, ignoring ridicule, he builds it anyway, and low and behold they do come.

Well, that was exactly my story. No one thought it was possible to run a successful business from out of my home. Heck, there was no such thing as a home business back then, let alone the technology and internet to support it. But just like Kevin Costner, I built my studio anyway and yes, they did come.

It is ironic how times have changed. Nowadays, mostly because of COVID, twenty-two million people are working from their home full time. And as Yoda from *Star Wars* might say, "Just a little ahead of my time, I was."

***

One of my first projects in my own studio turned out to be a blockbuster. I was asked to write a jingle for the *International Exposition Center* in Cleveland, Ohio; which is known as the *IX Center*. The complex welcomes more than two million visitors annually. It is a 2.2 million square-foot building and was recognized in the Guinness Book of World Records as the largest single-building convention center of its time.

But it's more than just space to accommodate trade shows. The building had an amusement park built inside of it with a full-scale Ferris wheel in the center. It had a large glass dome on top that allowed the Ferris wheel to extend through its roof. It was this amusement park that was the focus of the jingle.

The IX Indoor Amusement Park jingle with Billy Sullivan singing lead vocals and Ed Sarley on guitar became an iconic rite of Spring. And for a jingle that was only supposed to run for one year it had much greater staying power. It ran for twenty-four years. That's right, nearly a quarter of a century. That blows my mind. Just hearing someone say the words IX Indoor Amusement Park makes you immediately start to sing the tune.

Billy Sullivan who tours with Rich Spina and Peter Noone of Herman's Hermits is still asked to play it at every gig. When he plays it in Cleveland the crowd goes wild and they always sing along.

I was just thinking, the young kids that I had singing background vocals on the jingle are now all grown up. Some of them got married and have kids of their own who are now about the same age as they were when they sang the jingle. Boy, that really makes me feel old.

Anyway, I wrote the piece so that it would work its way into your brain, and you wouldn't be able to get it out. I must have done something right because Colleen Smitek in a *Cleveland Magazine* article noted:

...James Kellaris, a marketing professor at the University of Cincinnati hails the IX jingle as "A royal flush in earworm poker."

I loved what he said and how he characterized the jingle, but it was really very simple. Basically, it was two notes, repetitious, and had a hook that is absolutely annoying and you just can't stop singing it. Now what can be better than that?

Once I was sitting at a bar and the IX jingle started playing on the television. The guy sitting a couple of seats down from me slaps his beer down and loudly proclaims, "If I ever find the guy that wrote that... it's the most annoying thing I've ever heard."

As usual, with me just being me, I said, "Excuse me sir, that would be me."

Immediately he started to apologize and said, "I only meant annoying because I can't stop singing it in my head."

I told him, "There was no need to apologize and that saying it's annoying was actually a compliment."

To me it actually was. When writing a jingle, if it's annoying in terms of being memorable then it's a success and what I always strive for. The best part of the whole encounter was that he bought me a beer.

***

Writing music for the franchise called Ambiance, The Store for Lovers was a whole different experience from the *IX Indoor Amusement Park* jingle.

Henry and Jennifer, the owners were easy to work with and always had an adventure to share. They were clever and very successful, and had built their business franchise to include six stores within northeast Ohio.

When I first had the voice talent Diane come in to do the voice over, she looked at the script and I wasn't sure she was going to stay. The first line she had to read was "Come, to Ambiance." Sounds simple, right? Well, it wasn't the words per say, it was the directions on how to say it that made her feel uncomfortable.

They wanted the word "come" to be emphasized. Now, just think about that for a moment, the name of the store is Ambiance, the Store for Lovers. How do you think they wanted it emphasized? You guessed it, and so did Diane and that's what made things awkward. But being the trooper she is, she used her best sexy airy voice and she nailed it. She was now the new voice of Ambiance.

***

On a side note, once a client invited Janet and I to go on vacation to a Hedonism resort. Never having been to one we decided to do some research to see what it was all about. Boy, it was an eye-opener. Come to find out the resorts are lifestyle-friendly, clothing-optional beach resorts. That's right there is more than one. Who knew? Anyway, they went on to explain that you can do pretty much what you want, whenever you want. I should not have been surprised, just look at the name of the resort. Needless to say, we respectfully declined.

* * *

Not all clients were like the *IX Indoor Amusement Park* jingle or the commercials for Ambiance, the Store for Lovers. One of my biggest and longest running gigs was working with the accounting firm in downtown Cleveland called Ernst and Young, now known as E&Y. It definitely was a suit and tie place of business. I wondered how that first meeting was going to pan out with my ponytail and casual dress.

When I walked into their towering building in downtown Cleveland it was a little intimidating. It was a massive open space full of marble and windows. There was a guard dressed in his official finery sitting behind a massive desk. He looked at me, I'm sure thinking this guy is in the wrong building; and without even sitting up, and using a curt unaccommodating voice he said, "Can I help you?"

I told him my name and who I had an appointment with and immediately his attitude changed. He stood, welcomed me with a smile and said, "Good afternoon Mr. Sipl. Welcome to Ernst and Young. Please take the elevator to the fourth floor and someone will be there to greet you." And from that day forward, the guard always remembered me. Maybe it was the ponytail.

Ernst and Young had a beautiful video editing suite built in-house. The problem was they didn't have an in-house audio department. This was great news for me. Not only did I write original music for them, but I was their go-to-guy for any post to picture narration or special effects that were needed.

While working on the projects, I learned more than I ever wanted to know about accounting, finance and current tax laws. We created instructional videos that would inform their accountants of the current practices, forms, procedures, tips and tricks, as well as current tax changes. But one thing I learned for sure, I'm glad I'm not an accountant!

One of Ernst and Young's yearly activities is presenting an award called, *The E&Y Entrepreneur of the Year Award*, and it is given to a CEO or owner of a business that has shown outstanding leadership and entrepreneurship. It is presented at a formal event at the end of each year. It was started in 1986 in Milwaukee as a single award, but as of 2016 it has grown to twenty-five programs encompassing all fifty US states and more than sixty countries.

This end of year event is very much like any television awards show. It is this show that I wrote my original music for. To my surprise, the music I wrote for two of these shows won *Telly Awards*. The *Telly Award* showcases the best work created for television or video with entries from all 50 states and 5 continents. I have actually won four *Telly Awards* in total, and they are one of the most beautifully striking awards I have ever seen. They are tall, winged, sleek beauties. One of my favorites.

To add more icing to the cake, I also won a *US International Film and Video Festival Award*. It was for my music on a video I did for Ernst and Young called *Beat of the Entrepreneur.* So, as you can see, it is possible for a longhaired ponytailed kid from the west side of Cleveland to have a mutual and prosperous friendship with a not so stuffy accounting firm.

***

Another very lucrative corporate client that I wrote music for was Boeing. Their headquarters were in Seattle, Washington at the time so I was totally surprised when they called me. They are the leading global aerospace company in the world. They develop, manufacture and service commercial airplanes, defense products and space systems in more than 150 countries. They had heard my name and my music. They thought we would be a good fit. Of course, I said, "Yes."

I wrote original music for all their corporate videos introducing new jets and other defense or space system products. I was also writing music for videos which promoted their company dynamics. No matter what it was: writing original music, adding anything post to video such as sound effects, or doing over dubs or assemblies, they would get a finished product from me. Again, it was the all-in-one package of skills that I could offer them and they loved it.

I can't imagine the cost of the products they were selling, which of course was never divulged in the videos. It must have been a pretty penny and then some because the videos were first class advertising. Always a step above and beyond. Over the years, Boeing and I did many projects together and had a very prosperous relationship. It was a pleasure to work with them.

As with all my long-term clients when you work with someone repeatedly both parties get comfortable with each other's process, mindset and needs. It makes working with that client productive, easy and fun. Some even get to the point of handing you the product and saying, "Just do your thing, you know what to do."

It reminds me of when Jimmy Ienner told me, "To just do what needs to be done," when working on *Hungry Eyes* for the *Dirty Dancing* movie. It's a show of confidence in my judgement and skills. Developing this level of credibility is only built over time, and having this level of confidence in a person is a critical part of success.

***

There was one project that although it was small it was close to my heart. I was asked to do a proposal for Mercer County, Pennsylvania. They wanted a jingle promoting their county.

The meeting was held in Sharon, Pennsylvania. Sound familiar? Sharon is where I was born. The day of the meeting just happen to be on my fiftieth birthday. No way was I going to change that meeting date. It was providence working double time on this one! With providence's help or not, I got the job and I got to visit the town I was born in. It was an amazing day. It's the little things that make life special.

***

Another amazing day happened when I got a phone call from a friend. It all started many years ago when I worked with John Waite at After Dark Studio. It was so long ago I had actually forgotten.

John Waite was the former lead singer of the bands Babys and Bad English and is well known for his #1 smash hit *Missing You*. He loves the Cleveland area having lived in Northfield, Ohio when he first came to the United States. I knew him from working with him at After Dark Studio. He had just started on his solo career.

I remember he thought the Agora was great and he loved the whole rock and roll atmosphere of Cleveland. He thought it was a perfect place for a young rock musician. He said it felt like home to him. He was fantastic to work with and we really got along, but I really didn't think too much more about it. He was a talented musician and singer, who had great ideas, listened to other people's ideas and made great music. Who could ask for more!

Then one day a friend calls me and tells me, "John Waite, is on the radio, and just talked about you in an interview." They had asked John about his time living in the Cleveland area. John said, "He has a strong love for Ohio, because it was the first place he came to in the United States."

The person interviewing John, then asked him, "If anyone or anything in Ohio had an influence on him or his music."

He thought for a moment and said, "Well yes, as a matter of fact a guy named George Sipl taught me some great tips and tricks when we were working together at After Dark Studio in Cleveland."

WOW, I was blown away. Just goes to show, you never know when your everyday actions will leave an impression on someone. It is an amazing thrill to have anyone say that you had an impact on them. But to have someone of John Waite's talent and success to say that you made a difference means so much. Thank you, John.

The Jingle Man

George Sipl is the creator of the infamous I-X Indoor Amusement Park jingle. Do you hate him already?

To succeed, you must annoy people.

Such is the life of a jingle writer. In Cleveland, there is perhaps no greater success than George Sipl, the creator of the tune used to hype the I-X Indoor Amusement Park. In fact, we're willing to bet that mere mention of the annual event already has the song barreling through your head: "It's here today. Not gonna stay. Let's go to the I-X Indoor Amusement Park."

Image 109A: **Beginning of a *Cleveland Magazine* Article.**
I loved it!

Image 109: Above: **Build my first home studio in our home** in Olmsted Falls, Ohio.

Image 110: Below: **Myself and Billy Sullivan on a T.V. interview for the IX Indoor Amusement Park.**

Image 111: Above: **John Waite**. I worked with John just after he left the English band The Babys.

Image 112: Below: **Telly Awards**, The 3 statues on the right. They are all for original music I wrote. One project was for the live *E&Y Entrepreneur of the Year Award Show*.

19
PUT-IN-BAY

仝仝仝

We decided to build a summer home in Put-In-Bay, Ohio. We had friends that lived on the island, some were full-time residents while others would just go up for the summer. Janet's friend Naomi and her husband Ron who she knew from working at Baldwin Wallace University had a summer place there and our new house was just around the corner from them. My friend John Webster, best known for his former work with John Lanigan and Jimmy Malone on WMJI, also lived close to us. John Webster could be quirky at times. He would often cut his Put-in-Bay lawn on his riding mower in the nude. Good thing the house was back off the road in the woods. (RIP my friend)

Having a summer home on the island was great. When bands that we knew were playing at the Bay, some would come over and stay with us instead of in the band house. They knew there was always a place for them with us that was air-conditioned and clean. A big step up from any band house.

We were also able to secure a dock for our boat. We docked at a tiny marina that was next to the Jet express. Sadly, things do change. The marina took out some docks to make room for jet skis, and now restaurants and bars take up space where the marina office use to be. I guess that's progress.

Because Janet taught school and was off all summer; she and our two westies would stay at the Bay full time. I would come to the Bay on Thursday afternoon and leave for home on Tuesday morning. But I could also work at the Bay. Some of my client's music or should I say project ideas were written while sitting on the deck with my guitar in hand. It really was inspirational.

Talking about inspirational, I remember Alex Bevin sitting on the deck on a quiet morning playing his guitar and singing as we had breakfast overlooking the garden. It doesn't get any better than that!

The home we build was a three-bedroom ranch, with two baths, a fireplace and a huge deck. We also had a hot tub installed; which as I am writing this brings up a lot of stories I really should share.

Anyway, we built the home to accommodate a lot of company and we loved having everyone come and stay. We always had people coming and going. Everyone was always welcome. The largest group we had at one time was ten people. As I remember it not one person made it to work that Monday. Sorry, not my fault.

We even bought a car just for the Island, a 1980 Dodge Omni Miser. We called it our "Island Rat." We kept it on the island just to make it easy when we had to pick up guests from the ferry which was almost every weekend. Most of the time Janet and I used a two-person scooter to get around. It made it easier to maneuver around all the golf carts and cars.

Weekdays were always quiet and the best time to be there, but weekends could be a nightmare with traffic and the tourists. They weren't always on their best behavior.

***

Since I'm speaking about Put-In-Bay tourists, now would be the best time to share our weekend at the Bay hot tub story. Janet was at the Bay alone on a Friday night, which didn't happen often. She heard noises outside of the bedroom window and the dogs started barking. She looked out the window and there were four drunk people in our hot tub, two guys and two girls.

She called the police, put on a robe and went outside. Using her best "don't mess with me" teacher persona, she succinctly addressed the situation. They had broken the lock on the hot tub to get in it. They had no clothes on and they were loudly singing and drinking beer. They had beer cans tossed all over including some floating in the tub.

Janet said, "Excuse me, just what do you think you are doing?"

They instantly stopped singing, turned their heads toward her and with the biggest silly grins on their faces said, "HI."

One of the guys who was trying to spit out a full sentence slurred out the words, "We didn't think you would mind."

Staying calm she firmly directed them, "You need to get out of the tub, and do it NOW!"

With their smiles gone they got out of the tub. The whole-time whimpering, "You are a very mean lady." They grabbed their clothes and started to walk away, trying to put their clothes back on as they were walking.

And that's when my dear wife Janet's best sounding teacher's voice and persona materialized. She instructed them calmly but succinctly saying, "Whoa, just a minute. You guys come back here, clean up your beer cans and put the cover back on the hot tub."

And to her surprise they did just that; all the while still mumbling how mean she was. The police showed up two hours later. So much for police protection on the bay.

***

Another weekend, I was playing at the Round House with Rock Shop. It was Don Krueger, Jeff Scarborough, Laura Van and myself. The stage was so tiny at the Round House that I had to prop my one foot on the edge of the stage so I wouldn't fall off. After the gig everyone came over and we drank and had a great time until the sun started to come up. I remember Donny sitting in the hot tub talking. Then the next thing we knew he would be sleeping and slowly slipping under the water. We would grab him and pull him up to keep his head above water. He would cough, sputter a few words and then before we knew it, down he would slide again. The next day we did find his glasses at the bottom of the hot tub unbroken. Thank goodness both he and his glasses survived.

***

In the winter time we would fly over and spend some weekends at the Bay. Everything was closed except one bar where everyone went. This made it easy to get to know the people who were permanent residents. We would go up for the New Year's dinner and party. It was a real learning experience. It was such a small group and you had to be careful what you said. At one time or another everyone seems to have dated one another or even been married to another islander. So, we were always careful about not taking sides in island disputes and absolutely no gossip. We would just listen and smile.

***

We had neighbors that were permanent residents so they would keep an eye on our house all winter. We had a thermostat that would call us if the temperature went below a certain degree, but we had an aquarium that needed to be checked on once in a while. We had a self-feeder but what we didn't count on is that the water in the aquarium kept evaporating. So, we decided to fly up put the fish in coolers and use hand warmers to transport them back to the mainland. It was a success. No fish perished and our friends Bob and Maxie didn't have to fill the aquarium every other day. Live and learn.

***

We had our summer home at the Bay for just over five years. Then one day I was sitting at a bar on the mainland and I ran into someone I knew from Put-in-Bay.

Out of the blue the guy says, "I really want to buy your place at the Bay."

I was stunned and told him, "It's not for sale."

He said, "Well give me a call if you ever change your mind."

When I went home, I told Janet about what he said. I had mix feeling. I really didn't want to sell but I wasn't sure we should miss this opportunity.

191

She said, "Well, make him an offer so ridiculously high that he won't take it. Then we won't have to decide to sell or not. He can make the decision for us. If he takes it, then good for us. It's a win-win situation all the way around."

So, we made an offer that would give us more than double what we thought we would ever get from selling it. Without a second thought he took it. Bingo, it was decided and we moved on. It couldn't have happened at a better time. I had been in my studio for eleven years and I now needed a bigger studio.

We decided to use the capital gains to build a new home with a larger studio for me. Just goes to show how wrong all those "helpful" people were with their negative comments about how my home business would not work out. You don't know unless you try, and as Kevin Costner said in the movie, "Built it and they will come," and they did. Now it was time for a larger studio.

Image 113A: Above **Put-In-Bay Airport**: Easy access to the airport during the winter months. Airport was across the street from our home on Put-In-Bay.

Image 113 Above: **Our summer home at Put-In-Bay.**
Our bedroom window next to the hot tub.

Image 114: Below: **Alex Bevan Troubadour extraordinaire.**

Image 115: Above **Round House Bar**: The stage was so small it was hard for all four band members to fit on it.

Image 116: Below: **Round House Bar at Put-In-Bay, Ohio**.

20
NEW HOME STUDIO

全仝全

It had now been more than eleven years since I started my own business. It was going well and more clients were now coming to the house for sessions so a larger studio with an area and a desk for the client was needed. Mortgage rates were good and we knew our current home would sell with no problem. We started looking and found the perfect builder. The development is called Lake Isaac Reserve in Middleburg Heights, and we could build the house to our specifications.

I wanted to make sure the house was sound proof. I certainly didn't want my new neighbors getting mad. My buddy Stein Mesich, his wife Kathy, Janet and I insulated every floor, ceiling and wall inside and out. I did it for soundproofing but it also made a huge difference in my heat and air-conditioning bills. We also finished the basement ourselves. Stein is an expert craftsman but he also knows the music business. He was the guitar tech for some high-level bands including Twisted Sister and Cheap Trick. It was good to be working with someone so skilled and had an understanding of recording constraints. We built the whole studio ourselves. We even had the glass on the sound booth tilted at the proper angle so sound didn't bounce back. Besides the walls and ceilings and floor I also put-up extra sound deadening acoustic tiles.

We really worked well as a team, except when Stein accidentally shot Janet from across the room with the nail gun. Good thing she had on extra tight jeans because it bounced off with nothing but a small red mark. She was really lucky.

The finished studio was amazing. It was definitely larger than what I had before. It has a dedicated sound booth; a separate client area and the whole studio is completely soundproof. I was delighted. The location of the house also worked out well. It was close to all major highways. It has easy access to the Turnpike, Interstate 71 and 480, as well as the airport which makes it great for clients coming in from out of town.

The house itself backs up to the Metro Parks with trees and wildlife galore. It is definitely a park-like setting. Clients always mention how they love to come to my home studio. It may be the relaxed welcoming feel, or our two cute westies that greet every client at the door. Of course, It may even have been my technical skills. You just never know! Anyway, I'm just glad they came. All-in-all the move was definitely the right choice.

The new home allowed space for a grand piano. I also had room to put in a home theater with a ten-foot screen, surround sound and six reclining theater chairs. It is great for screening videos that I work on as well as for watching movies. I challenge anyone to try and watch a movie without falling asleep. Everyone who comes to enjoy a movie for the first time usually ends up sleeping because the chairs are so comfortable.

How do I know they fall asleep? SNORING! I have even recorded a few because they didn't believe me. Just goes to show never fall asleep at a sound engineer's house. They may record you snoring.

On a side note, we have currently lived in our home for over twenty-four years. When retirement came, we decided to stay in a home we love. Who knows how many more years we have, but planning ahead we put an elevator in the house. It can accommodate three people or two people and a wheelchair. And with my studio being at home, I can still work whenever I want even through retirement. It was the perfect solution to not having to move. We now get to stay in a home and studio we both love.

Image 117A: **Stein Mesich and myself.** My partner in crime when building. We make a great team.

Image 117: Above: **Our new home where I built my new home studio.**

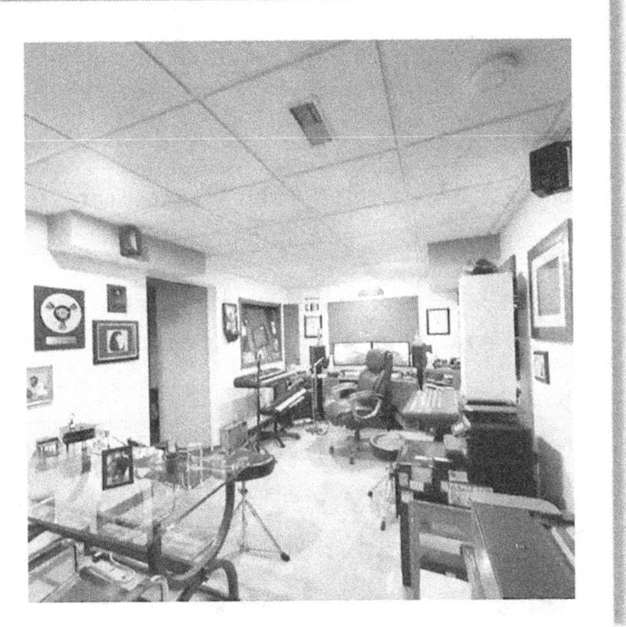

Image 119: Above **My new home studio** with sound booth, 2 computer monitors, surround speakers, mixing board, and a client desk.

Image 120: Below: **Client sitting area with a client desk.**

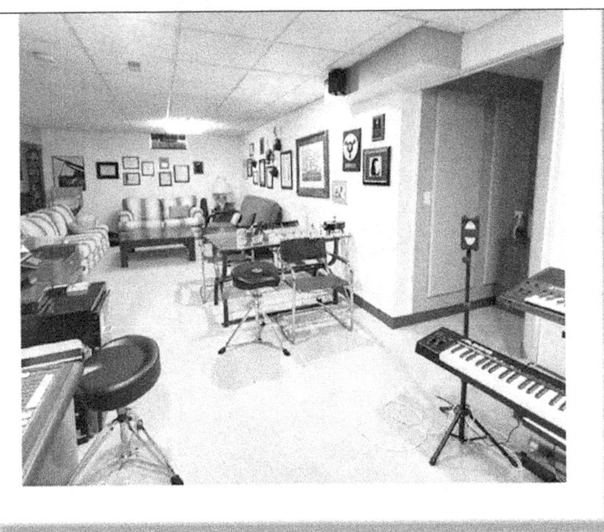

Image 121: Below right: **My new business cards for the new studio.**

Image 122: Below left: **New stationary for the new studio.** So cool to own your own company and have your own letterhead.

21
INFOMERCIALS

全全全

Now let's talk infomercials. According to Will Kenton of the website Investopedia, "An infomercial is a longer-form video or television advertisement that acts as a stand-alone program to pitch goods or service with a call to action. Infomercials are different from regular commercials because they last longer and have no breaks in the program." Which in my terms means... it's very long and calls for a shit load of music.

Many of the infomercials were about products that were created or promoted by Tony Little. He is somewhat of a Health & Fitness Guru that seemed to invent a new health machine every few months. Some of his infomercial products that I did music for were: EZ Glider, Gazelle, EZ Shaper, Super Trainer, as well as the Tony Little/Hometics Pillow. His commercials all were high energy with a lot of yelling in them, so the music had to present the same feel.

Back then exercise infomercials seemed to be the trend. All but one of the twenty or so Fitness Quest infomercials I wrote music for were some sort of an exercise machine or health product.

From the Ab Lounge, Ab Robic, Ab Supreme, Bio Force, BOSO Ball, Circle Glide, Pilates Power Gym, Rock Fit, Spin Mop, Zumba videos, and including all the Tony Little products, it's been a fun and lucrative relationship. I even got 4,000,000 units sold award from Ab Lounge. I guess that's the gold record of infomercials.

But I did receive a Mobius Advertising Award for the music I wrote in a Fitness Quest BioForce Infomercial. The award was originally established to honor national television commercials and was then expanded to include all forms of advertising media including infomercials.

I have come to realize that advertising people really love their awards. But I'm glad because it is always nice to get recognition for your work.

Infomercials have pretty much died out. The internet has taken its toll on that industry, and mine. I haven't done an infomercial since 2013.

***

Not only did I write the music for infomercials; I was also in one. I had been gifted an Ab Lounge by Fitness Quest. Amazingly I moved five belt holes from using it. I sure couldn't do that now.

While at the gym in New Hampshire with my brother-in-law Greg, that infomercial for Ab lounge came on the very large television screen above the treadmills we were using. There, plastered across this huge screen was me working out on the Ab Lounge. We both laughed and my brother-in-law said, "No getting away from you, is there?"

I often hear my work when I am out and about but seeing my mug plastered across that screen felt really weird. That was strange because I never felt that way when I played on stage. Maybe it was my subconscious telling me that I just missed playing my music on stage. I needed to give that some more thought.

***

I also wrote the music for some exercise videos for kids. But for this project I also had to go and record the audio while they taped the video. Pat Murray, formally the Director of the Cleveland Indians Broadcasts was doing the video while I did the audio. I would then assemble all the parts and write the original music to match and enhance all the videos.

These videos were then be sold as an instructional exercise package meant for young children. Who would buy such a thing? Well, the focus group was teachers, fitness instructors, and even parents. The whole package became a successful franchise business. It had tailored exercises and educational programs to go beyond just improving a child's physical health. All four pillars of fitness: aerobic, strength, flexibility, and mindset were addressed in a fun and entertaining way, and my music had to reflect it all.

***

Between 2010 and 2016 I was the voice of T&A/Petro Service Plaza throughout the United States. Doing voiceovers was just another reinvention of myself. One step of my on-going journey of learning, growing and doing. It helps keep my mind young and refreshed.

My weekly script for them consisted of announcing the current specials and sales, as well as promoting the benefits of their service plaza. I did all this in a gravelly Wolfman Jack style voice. It would rip the hell out of my throat, but I loved doing it. Just ask me the next time you see me; I'll give you an earful of my Wolfman Jack.

I must admit, I had a unique experience when I stopped for gas at one of their plazas when driving across the United States. I went into the store not really thinking about anything special. My only priority was using the restroom. As I walked through the door, I suddenly heard my Wolfman Jack voice come over the speaker. It is one of my favorite voices to do and when I hear myself doing it, I always smile just a little.

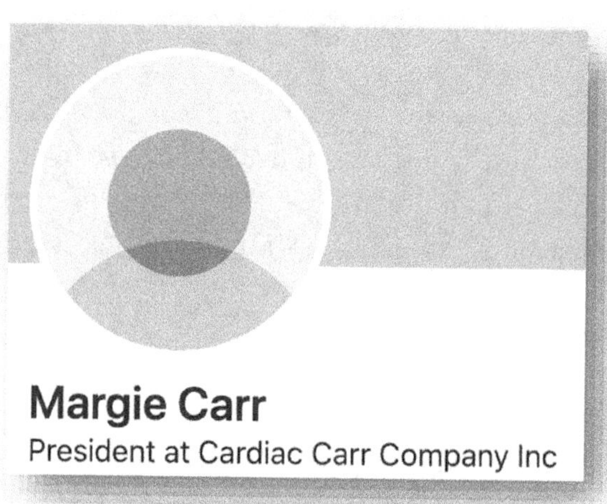

Image 123A: **Margie Carr** created the innovative cardiac exercise programs for children, which I wrote the original music for, engineered and played on.

Image 123: Above: **Yup, that's me in the 45-minute infomercial for Ab Lounge. I** wrote the music and used the product.

Image 123B: Below: **Won a Mobius Advertising Award** for music and engineering on a BioForce Video.

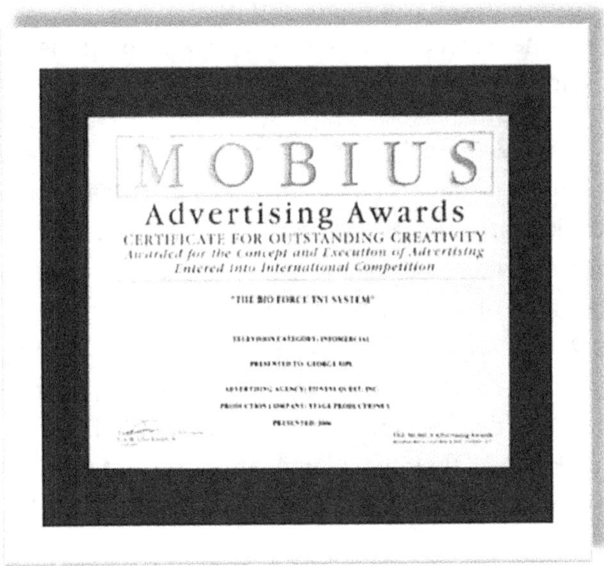

22

SPORTS, REALLY

全全全

Working with the Cleveland Cavaliers was very interesting considering I had never played any sports in or out of school. I always wanted to play but it never happened. Remember my parents! They were against me playing all sports because they were afraid that I might hurt my hands. Unfortunately, because of that mindset sports activities and I never interacted. This lack of familiarity with sports namely basketball made it awkward for me during my first meeting with the Cavs.

I went to Gund Arena in downtown Cleveland. It's the home of our Cleveland Cavaliers basketball team and now known as Rocket Mortgage Field House. It was my first meeting with Cavs management. It was awesome to be walking around seeing the players in their everyday clothes. I had only seen them on TV in their uniforms. I can't get over how big the players were. They towered over me. I really felt dwarfed and I'm almost six feet tall. When we shook hands, their hand would totally engulf mine. I bet that holding a basketball to them must be like me holding a softball. It was awesome and intimidating all at the same time.

When I took the elevator upstairs to the conference room, I was not sure what to expect. When the elevator doors opened things looked a little sterile. I walked down the hall and entered the conference room. This too had that same cold sterile feel. There were four people sitting around the table in casual business dress. They all stopped and smiled warmly. That made me feel a little more relaxed. I sat down with my ponytail and jeans and joined the meeting.

They were discussing the jumbotron and talking specifics about what type of sound effects would be most appropriate, as well as the timing for each one. After some discussion the head guy just stopped and looked at me.

I must have had a quizzical look on my face because he said, "You've never been to a game, have you?"

I had to admit I hadn't, and he said, "Wait just a minute," and he walked out of the room.

That was it, I was sure my days of writing music and doing sound effects for the Cavs were done. The next thing I knew he walked back into the room, slid two tickets across the table and said, "Here's two tickets, you need to see a game;" and so I did.

Janet and I went to see the Cavaliers play. We were sitting in the team's family section so the seats were great but that didn't make our experience any better. It was very much like a three ringed circus. Lights, video, music and sound effects were all coming from the jumbotron. Announcements were being made and of course the Cavs were playing basketball center court, but it seemed to be happening all at once. Like I said, a three ringed circus. We stayed for a while to make sure I had the gist of what I needed to do and then we left. I must say I enjoyed doing the sound effects and music for the jumbotron but that was the last game we ever went to and that was almost 20 years ago.

***

I have also written original music and done sound effects for other basketball teams such as the Washington Wizards, Denver Nuggets, and the Orlando Magic. All have huge arenas with their own jumbotrons. At the beginning of the game, there is a performance type of presentation, where they play music, make announcements, introduce the players, and the jumbotron goes crazy. It's this beginning of the game presentation that I created music for. It was very much like writing music for a jingle, only no words. Just like a jingle, it needed a hook and it had to be memorable, just what I was known for creating.

It seems like jumbotrons were turning up everywhere, and now they are found in most every sport's arena and stadium around the world. The jumbotron changed the way people view everything, from sporting events, to concerts, to even church services. It focuses attention to specific content or events, such as an instant replay, or even a fan in the stands, and often sound effects or music may be added. With this jumbotron technology becoming an essential part of so many venues, I was able to make this a lucrative part of my business, which is really ironic considering my history with sports.

***

But it is not just basketball teams I wrote music for. I also wrote for baseball teams. I was honored to write original music for the Cleveland Indians, now known as the Guardians, as well as writing music for the Baltimore Orioles. On a personal note, I do miss Chief Wahoo, and our former team's name, the Indians.

Anyway, the Baltimore Orioles have a huge jumbotron that also needed original music. The process was very much the same as writing music for the Cavaliers jumbotron, a wordless jingle. But it was different in the fact that baseball is played outdoors and during the summer so the music would have a different feel. The music was more Americana, and was a lot less glitzy or flashy than the basketball music. Even my choice of instruments would be different.

***

A special project that I did with the Cleveland Indians was a unique promotional video. It was totally different from anything I had ever done. It was a 3D video that was created to promote and help finance the new stadium for the Cleveland Indians.

When Jacob's Field, now known as Progressive Field, was being built the Cleveland Indians organization and the Gateway Economic Development Corporation worked closely to fund, design and build a world-class facility. They promoted the fact that it was created expressly for baseball and specifically for our Cleveland Indians. I just think that meant is was going to cost more!

The video was unique in that it was a virtual 3D video. It was something new for its time. It was shown on a large screen and it allowed the viewer to virtually enter the new stadium and have a 3D view of everything. From top to bottom the viewer was given the full tour. It even included a visual 3D fly by that made you duck when it happened. Well at least I ducked.

I was really proud of the end product and they loved it. Now that technology is used in everyday video games. Wow, technology has really changed our lives.

But for its time this project was cutting edge and I was proud to have won an International Award for my music on the video from the AMI, which is the Association for Multi-Media International. I also won an Exhibition of Excellence Award for a different piece of original music I wrote for a Cleveland Indians' video.

Yes, the Indians and I have had a long and prosperous relationship, which is odd considering my background with sports.

So, I guess I'll say that I am a sports fan in my own way. With my longtime friend Jim Stamper being the number one Indians baseball fan, how could I not be a fan? And like Jimmy, I also have had a hard time with the name change. Making the transition to calling them the Cleveland Guardians will take some time. But I'll keep working on it.

Image 126B: Above: **Jim Stamper's Tam O'Shanter Bar** was the place where all musician and Indians Baseball fans would hang out. Even Tom Hanks said it was his favorite place to go.

Image 126A: Above: **Jim Stamper. Number one Indians baseball fan.** Always had his Chief Wahoo with him at the games. Photo by Daniella Zalcman.

Image 126: Above: **Cavs jumbotron at Gund Arena**. Engineered, wrote music and created sound effects for the jumbotron.

Image 127: Below: **Cleveland Cavaliers Logo.**

Image 128, Image 129, Image 130: **Engineered, wrote music and created sound effects for the Orlando Magic, Denver Nuggets and Washington Wizards basketball teams.**

23

COMMERCIALS AND MORE

仝仝仝

***

It was great that so many of my clients, who I had written commercials and jingles for at Beachwood, had followed me to my own studio. Commercial spots and jingles are always exciting to do. You never know how long they will run or if they will get noticed. Not all of them have the impact or staying power of the *IX Indoor Amusement Park* jingle, which ran for almost a quarter of a century, but a few have come close.

Axelband and Brown, which is the ad agency that became Brown and Miller in Beachwood, brought me numerous clients that needed television spots and jingles. This included clients like Goo Gone, Mickey Mart, and Georgio's Oven Fresh Pizza Company. Can you guess which one was the hardest? You got It, the Georgio's Oven Fresh Pizza Company. It's a real mouthful and I don't mean the pizza. They wanted the whole title included. Just saying it I get tongue tied. Rhythmically it was almost impossible but I managed to fit it all in. Thank goodness they were happy with the final product.

***

I had worked on some Ohio Lottery spots when I was at Beachwood. I was fortunate that they followed me when I moved to my own studio. Apart from the commercial where I got to drive my Porsche over 100 mph, three of my favorite Lottery commercials were My Dad, Holiday Games, and the commercial Tickle. It still makes me laugh to think about the Tickle commercial to this today. Basically, the Tickle commercial was about giving your dad Lottery Tickets for Christmas instead of a scratchy wool sweater. The music had to be funny yet have an upbeat Christmas feel with over-the-top silly cartoon type sound effects. I remember having to create the scratchy wool sweater sound. You would be surprised how each fabric has its own sound. I scratch with the guy every time I see the video.

***

Another client that followed me from Beachwood was the HGTV's series *Room by Room*. The shows ran a half-hour long and I wrote original music that spanned the whole show. The music for each episode had to reflect the theme of that specific show. As I said before, working with Matt and Shari was always amazing; but what put the icing on the cake is that I won a Communicator Award for one of the shows. It's an international award for the music I wrote for the *Room by Room* episode called New England Bedrooms.

***

Not too long after I left Beachwood Elaine Rogalski whom I had worked with at Beachwood Studios/EDR, also decided to move on. She too opened her own business with her husband Vic Iacovone, called Novasphere. She had great people working for her including Lin Croskey. Elaine and I had worked on Burger King together at Beachwood Studios, and now we would be working on Burger King again. This time with each of us owning our own businesses. You can't get much better than that.

Working with Elaine I wrote original music for Sherwin Williams, Church's Chicken, Arby's and Heinz. All were internal corporate videos and shows. Our working relationship has developed into a bond of friendship, work and trust.

Just a quick story about my wife and Elaine. Janet has absolutely no musical talent and she freely admits it. But what she does have is an incredible Consumer's Ear for music. With all the projects I have done for Elaine, Janet is batting a thousand when it comes to knowing what the client and Elaine will like.

One time I had written this ethereal musical score. Faintly in the background I had birds periodically chirping.

My wife said, "I don't think Elaine is going to like the birds,"

I said, "They are so faint, she will probably never even hear them."

Well, I was so wrong. Elaine absolutely loved the music but she had one comment. That's right, she wanted the birds out. I should have known better than to go against my wife and her infallible Consumer's Ear for music. I can always count on Elaine asking, "What does Janet think?" Next time I'll remember.

***

Another client who followed me from Beachwood to my own studio was Debbie Richards of the Saifman and Richards Agency. She was the first person to ever ask me to write a post score for a corporate video at Beachwood Studios. At the time, it was definitely a step in a new direction that facilitated a very lucrative addition to my career. And then surprise it happened again. Debbie Richards brought me another very important project, but this time I was working at my own studio. Yet again, the project she brought me was a huge success. Thank you, Debbie!

This new project was a commercial for General Car Insurance. The jingle I wrote for them, *For the best car insurance rates in town, call 1- 800 General Now* has been running for over twenty-five years. It's the second commercial that I have written that has had this type of longevity, and that doesn't often happen. The other jingle that has been around forever is the *IX Indoor Amusement Park*. Unfortunately, the IX jingle is only known regionally, but the *1- 800 General Now* commercial is known nationally, getting much more exposure.

Companies will typically change ad agencies trying to get a fresh take on promoting their product. But if their company jingle already has a memorable hook that identifies that product then they really don't want to change it. Yet, they will still ask for something new and different. Welcome to the world of advertising. They want change but they don't. Makes it hard to write jingles for this kind of mindset. Yet I do it often. It's just part of the business.

What was great about the General commercial was that when I wrote it, I was starting with a blank slate. I could write whatever I wanted, and I did. Seeing that they had created a visual of a general to represent their company, I wanted to keep a military feel in the music I wrote. The military cadence really lends itself to rap music, so that's the direction I decided to go. Keeping that cadence in mind I wrote, *For the best car insurance rates in town, call 1-800 General Now.*

It was good, but I wanted to add one more thing that would draw attention to it and hook the consumer. I decided to put two referee sounding whistles just before the jingle starts. The two whistles are part of the rhythm and act as the first two beats. It really worked out well. When the consumer hears the two whistles the whole jingle immediately jumps into their head. It was a success all the way around.

As I stated before, companies change ad agencies, and the ad agency always want change. But it's really hard to try and change something that is so recognizable. So, what they do is try to keep the memorable part but change the rest. They even tried to change the original voice that I used to say the tag line in the General commercial. That didn't work and they went back to using Rick Sellers, the voice-over that I originally recorded. My jingle may have been shifted and shaped in many different ways but it always has that familiar hook that I first wrote.

***

As I mentioned before, one of my longer running jingles was for Spitzer's car dealership. I wrote music for their 85th Anniversary commercial. It was this musical hook that turned into *Spitzer, Our World Revolves Around You,* and it is still running today in some form or another. I can tell it has been taken to other ad agencies and they have played around with the music. But as they always seem to do, they came back to the same original music I wrote with its memorable hook. As soon as you hear it, you will sing not say the words: *At Spitzer, Our World Revolves Around You.* I'm humming the tune for you right now.

***

USA Insulation is a jingle I wrote in 2011 for the Ad Agency called All Media Design. It started out as a local commercial and now it has gone national. While I was in Atlanta, I was surprised to hear the jingle running on Television. I'm glad the company is growing and still using my jingle. It really must have been a good fit.

***

A project completely different from the commercials I had been writing was creating music for Cleveland's Bicentennial and Their Bridge Lighting Ceremony in downtown Cleveland. Eight bridges were lit and each bridge had a different lighting theme. They were meant to be permanent features and to stay lit for the next century.

Bob Hope came back to Cleveland, his hometown. He was the grand marshal of the Parade of Boats and he pull the ceremonial switch to turn the bridge lights on. It was a special moment for him and for Cleveland, The City of Bridges.

219

A corresponding video was created to be played during the lighting ceremony. It was shown on huge jumbotron type screens throughout the city. I was asked to write the music for it. Its purpose was to create a sense of pride in Cleveland's rich history and bright future. The video featured aerial shots of downtown Cleveland and its bridges. It also included Cleveland landmarks, as well as close-ups of people living, working and playing downtown and in the Flats.

The video editor did a fantastic job of arranging the images. I was able to follow the flow and feel of what the images were trying to convey. It was important for me to reflect their story in the music. I created different sections or movements. The beginning had a crisp industrial feel; and as directed by the pulse of the images the music continued to build. Reflecting the final sequence of images, the music built to a crescendo which then led to the finale.

I really thought the original music I wrote for this video was one of my best projects. But the presentation on that night was not advantageous to what the music and video were all about. It was supposed to create a sense of pride in Cleveland's rich history and future. Instead, the whole event was just an excuse for a huge party with a lot of drinking and hooting and hollering. WOW, it sounds like I'm venting. Well, I guess I am.

When the jumbotron screens were activated during the lighting ceremony and the video was being shown, it seemed like it was a signal for a party to begin. Like a light switch being turned on, people let out a big cheer, made toasts, drank beer and continued to whistle and scream. Maybe at some of the other vantage points around the city it may have been different, but from where we were stationed it was just time to party.

So, even though the original music that I wrote for the video was a success technically, as well as being emotionally impactful, I was disappointed in the overall presentation and use of the finished project. No aspiring musician or veteran performer wants their music to be unheard and that is exactly what happened here.

***

On an opposite note, the music I wrote for the Cleveland Clinic video on Empathy has received over 6.9 million views and still counting. This project started as a single in-house corporate video, and has become a focal point for building a human connection to patient care through empathy; connecting mind, body and soul.

The video is special in the fact that not one word is spoken throughout the video. It is just images and music. Each person has a caption explaining the circumstances for them being in the hospital. Whether they are there working or just visiting, for a birth or a death, feeling happy or sad, all of their emotions are reflected in the music and it is very impactful.

I still get a chill thinking about specific situations portrayed in the video. There is one that shows a mother and daughter in the lobby of a hospital slowly walking with their heads down. Then with a faint smile on the daughter's face they stop to pet the therapy dog. A caption drifts in next to the mother saying "Husband is dying," and then the caption slowly fades out while the piano is plucking at your heart. A new caption fades in next to the girl, saying, "Going to see her dad for the last time." OMG, now your heart starts to cry. I cannot tell you how emotional it was to write that music, and even more impactful to sit and watch it and listen to what I wrote. You cannot watch it without feeling great emotion. Needless to say, I am extremely proud of this music. The fact that it has been seen by over 6.9 million people is mind-boggling to me.

I was very honored to receive an international award from the Cannes Corporate Media and Television Awards for the music I wrote on the Empathy video. This award annually honors corporate films, online media productions and documentaries throughout the world. The event takes place in one of the most important film centers in the world Cannes, France.

It amazing to realize that this first born American from a small town in Pennsylvania who had three fingers of his right hand cut off and reattached is competing with other professionals from around the world. Winning recognition for music I wrote, engineered, produced and performed is great. It doesn't get much better than that. But just keeping it real, it's really just icing on the cake. Awards are not what success is all about.

***

While writing this book I had to take stock of what music I had written, who I wrote the music for and if I had won any awards doing it. I was surprised that I didn't recall some of the projects I engineered or wrote music for or even some of the awards that I had won. It seems strange that I forgot about something I created. I guess some projects are just not as impactful as others; and not all projects can be as memorable to me as the Empathy video.

It is always nice to receive recognition or an award. But over the years I have come to realize that receiving that outside acclaim is not what success and happiness is all about. Rather it is when I can satisfy my inner drive as I go through my journey of learning, growing and doing.

I know that I have been full of musical dreams since I was a child, and have gradually emerged as a unique musician in terms of how I have chosen to apply my musical talent. I have been successful both professionally and financially. But one thing I know for sure about acclaim and platitudes, they are not what life is all about.

The 6.9 million views of the Empathy video give me the greatest satisfaction. The people who view it don't know that I wrote the music or won an award for it. They just know they liked the video and by word of mouth the news spread and so did the views. That is what really makes me feel fulfilled.

Image 124A: **Georgio's Oven Fresh Pizza Co.**
I wrote the jingle for their commercial. It's a real mouthful.

Image 124 and Image 125: **Award for Composing and Arranging the music for the HGTV Series *Room by Room*.**

Image 131: Above: **Cleveland Ohio Bicentennial Bridge Lighting Ceremony**. I wrote and arranged the music for the Lighting Ceremony's presentation video.

Image 132: Below: **Bob Hope was the Grand Marshal of Cleveland's Bicentennial Parade**. He threw the switch to light the bridges.

Image 133: Above: ***Cleveland Clinic's Empathy video.*** I wrote, arranged and performed the music for this video. It has over 6.9 million views on you tube.

Image 134: Below: From **Cannes, France a *Corporate Media & TV Award*** for composing, arranging and performing the music on the *Cleveland Clinic Empathy* Video.

Image 135: Above: **Wrote the jingle for USA Insulation commercial.**

Image 136: Below: **I wrote the jingle for the General Insurance Commercial.**

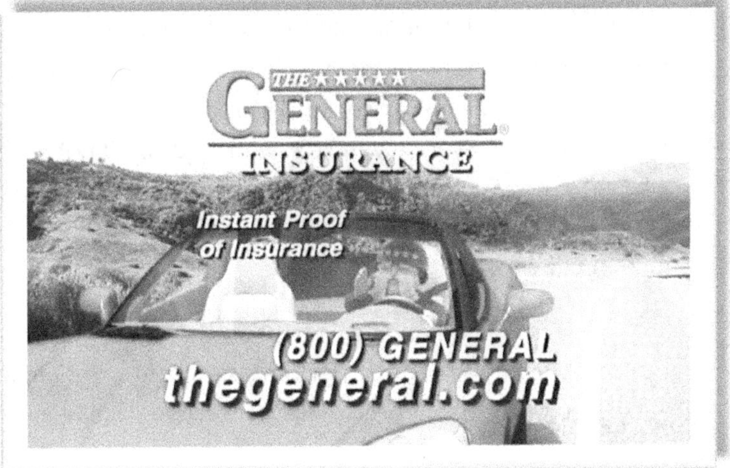

24

IMPACT

全全全

It's going to seem that this whole next chapter has been devoted solely to Impact Communications. Well, almost all! They are a multimedia company in downtown Cleveland that specializes in video and corporate events. I have been working with Impact since I first started engineering over forty years ago. In fact, I am still working with them to this day, even though I'm supposed to be retired. The number of projects has been prolific and is still growing.

As they so rightly proclaim on their website, "Impact is home to some of the most talented creatives in Cleveland." Bob MacDonald the head of the company, has put together a great team. From Irene Majer, Erika Robertson, Sue Finley, Kristy Somerlot, and my latest partner in crime Sydney Van Leeuwen, you could not ask for a better crew. Everything this group touches turns to gold. The USS Midway Museum project was just one of these golden endeavors.

This major exhibit was built on the lower deck of the USS Midway aircraft carrier that is presently docked in San Diego Harbor, California. This interactive display became a permanent part of the museum. It tells the story of the Battle of Midway, which was a major battle in the Pacific during World War II. It was a five-day battle where the Americans defeated the Japanese navy, and that changed the course of the war in the Pacific.

My main job was to create the audio for the full-scale engine room that was built within the museum. People could walk through this engine room and experience the exact moment it was being hit by a torpedo. The space itself was very authentic and impressive with its detail. We had to remember that many of the visitors would actually be servicemen. We had to be accurate down to the kind of nuts and bolts that were used.

Getting the correct sound effects for the different types of aircraft was precise and difficult. American aircraft engines had a beefier sound. Whereas the Japanese planes had a buzzing sound like that of a two-cycle engine. Soldiers were trained to know the difference so I had to get it right.

The audio installation was a four-channel sound system. Three of the four channels would carry the audio of flames flaring, people yelling, water rushing, and of all the other chaos that might ensue during an attack. Two speakers were placed in front of the visitors and one behind them. This was done so that they really felt surrounded by the chaos and would experience the panic. The final speaker was placed up and behind the visitors with the captain shouting commands through the ship's PA system.

Separate subwoofers were placed under the floor of where the people would walk. These subwoofers would not only create deep booming sounds during explosions, but it would vibrate the floor giving the illusion of really being hit with a torpedo.

I also created the audio for the kiosks that were placed around the exhibit. They told the history of the battle. They gave background facts about the ships and the people on them. There was also a theater that had a 3D hologram explaining what happened during the battle. Everything was a step up and beyond.

***

What was so great about this project, was that the USS Midway Museum flew Janet and me out to San Diego to see the grand opening. All the big money donors were at this event. So, there was no holds barred in what was provided. I was speechless.

They had set up food stations everywhere. When I say food stations, it was more like individual cafés. They had shrimp, lobster and prime rib. Each being served in its own area. There were attendants and/or a chef at each station. You could go back as many times as you wanted, and I did!

Of course, they had open bars providing only the best. Top shelf wine and liquor flowed like water. And since we only had to walk across the street to our hotel, we let it flow.

Now, if there was any room left in anyone's stomach, which there was not, the dessert stations looked decadent. Even if I did have some room, it would have been impossible to eat one small piece of every dessert offered. If you did, you would have exploded.

Janet decided to test it out. She was able to get through quite a lot of the desserts without exploding. Since she didn't explode, we decided we could stay a couple of extra days. We would make it a mini vacation. We were already in California; so why not?

***

The next day we rented a car. We thought a good place to eat lunch would be Yuma, Arizona. It was only two and a half hours to get there and we could take some fantastic photos on the way. Both Janet and I sell our photography and art work. We always have around 30 pieces hanging at a coffee shop gallery called Perk Cup Café in Berea, Ohio. So, off we went to Yuma.

Our first stop in Yuma was the historic Yuma Territorial State Prison. It is one of the most haunted prisons in the United States. I am not a believer in ghosts, but on the other hand I am not an unbeliever. My point of view is that our human form is energy with lots of synapses and cells exchanging energy. Science tells us that energy doesn't dissipate; it just changes form. The energy has to go somewhere, why not as a spirit? Maybe not, maybe so... No one really knows for sure. For those who do believe or for those who don't, just go and experience it yourself. It was spooky to say the least.

We then stopped at Lutes Casino in downtown Yuma. It is one of Yuma's oldest bars, over 100 years old. When we sat down at the bar, we saw an older white-haired gentleman. He was dressed in a white shirt with red garters around his arms and he sported a straw brimmed hat. He walked over to this old upright piano, sat down and adjusted his seat. Then, like someone had struck him with a lightning bolt he started playing ragtime. His fingers were flying across those keys and he played with his whole body. He was really enjoying himself. He was into every note he was playing, and so were we. I think we enjoyed watching him as much as we loved to listen to him. We found out that Lutes Casino is known for their Jazz Festival every summer. It sounds interesting.

The memorabilia at Lutes should not be missed. It is unusual and amazing. The Pee-wee Herman doll is a prime example of its quirkiness. But it would have taken a lifetime to see and get the story behind everything there. Unfortunately, we didn't have time. We needed to get going. It was another two-and-a-half-hour drive back.

***

The whole experience of being invited to see something I worked on was very special to me. It was nice to be able to see my work in a real time setting. It doesn't happen often. So much of my work is corporate meetings and events and I don't get invited to those.

But there was one other event where I did get an invite. It was a lot closer to home than the Midway project. It was right in downtown Cleveland. A big donor event hosted by the Cleveland Museum of Natural History.

As you have probably already guessed, this was another one of Impact's projects. And like the Midway Museum exhibit *The Cleveland Museum of Natural History's Ohio Rocks* display in their Smead Discovery Center was a hit.

The Ohio Rocks exhibit is one of those projects that was super interesting and fun to do. I also learned a whole lot about Geology. It involved writing songs for different geological time periods throughout early history including the Devonian, Mississippian, Cambrian, Silurian and more. The songs were not easy to write. You try to rhythmically rhyme something with Mississippian. It may not have been easy, but it was loads of fun and laughs.

I got to work with some fantastic singers and musicians like Alicia Burton, Billy Sullivan from Herman Hermits, Lynn Jarrell, Paul Sidoti who is Taylor Swifts guitar player and Wallace Coleman just to name a few.

The appeal of the songs was geared toward kids. The songs were educational, yet at the same time needed to hook their interest immediately. Hooking them was so important. We didn't want them to miss any of those exciting facts about that time period. One of my favorites was about the Mississippian Period. The song goes on to explain that fossils are found in sandstone, silt and shale. And in Ohio we can find these fossils in what we call Mississippian Mud pies.

I still remember the tag lines I wrote that ran through and linked together all nine songs;

Ohio Rocks, Lookin' at Ohio Rocks

Lookin' at our past

Come along and see

We're a lot different than we use to be

Ohio, Ohio Rocks.

Along with the Ohio Rocks Exhibit, I also did the audio for the entire Cleveland Museum of Natural History's handheld audio tours. These self-guided tours, were very high tech for their time. It was an option many museums were starting to utilize for their visitors. This in turn meant a lot of business for me.

***

I also recorded and assembled the audio tours for two of the Hyde Park Trail sites in New York. These included the home of Franklin D. Roosevelt and the Vanderbilt Mansion. The Hyde Park Trails System links three National Historic Sites, the FDR's Estate, Eleanor Roosevelt's Val-Kill and the Vanderbilt Mansion.

Museum work has been good to me. But it's not just the audio tours. From Kiosks, SFX, assemblies, voice overs, to writing original music, museum projects are interesting as well as profitable.

***

Some of my work with Impact consists of working with the same clients on a yearly basis; as is the case with Sterling Jewelers, Aspen Dental, and the Nestle Minor Awards Show. For Sterling Jewelers, now called Signet, I write the music for lyrics they give me. It kind of feels like an Elton John working with Bernie Taupin, but not.

One year, I even won a *Communicator* Award for the music I wrote for a Sterling show. I have also received two *Telly* awards for my music on The Beach Brook Video, and a Western Reserve Historical Society video. I do love the look of those *Telly* Awards.

Aspen Dental was an entirely different story. It was a video for their in-house national corporate meeting. It had Aspen Dental doctors, hygienists, dental assistants and receptionists across the United States singing the same pop song via GoPro cams. Then some of the stronger singers were flown to Chicago Recording studio in Chicago, or to Audio Works Digital studio in Cleveland to record the same song individually. I then took the tracks decided which ones to use. It was much like what was done on the *We Are the World* video. I finally ended up mixing sixty-four tracks, and using a lot of Autotune!

***

On the other hand, the yearly Nestle Minor Awards show, which I did from 2004 to 2015, consisted of recording Chefs being interviewed, and then the audio assembly. One particular Chef named Rocco, had been nominated twice but had never won.

He was the head Chef in the Union Oyster House in Boston which opened in 1826. It is the oldest restaurant in Boston, as well as the oldest restaurant in continuous service across the United States. It is full of memorabilia from Daniel Webster to the Kennedys. During the American Revolution many of our founding fathers frequented the establishment. Isaiah Thomas even published his newspaper "The Massachusetts Spy," from the second floor. The Spy is oldest newspaper in the United States. A lot of history in that restaurant.

Anyway, while in Boston Janet and I, along with her brother and sister-in-law, stopped by Union Oyster House for lunch and to say hello to Rocco. Unfortunately, it was his day off. But when the bartender called him at home to tell him we had stopped by, Rocco said he was sorry he missed us. He thanked us for stopping by and told the bartender to take care of us. Everything was on the house. It was wild.

They even had a special Sam Adams Brewery draft beer made only for them; damn, that was good. It really was a fantastic day. To this day, not sure how we safely made it back to New Hampshire that night. It took all four of us to drive.

Image 148: **Outside the Union Oyster House in Boston Massachusetts.**

Image 146: Above Logo: **Nestle Minor Awards Interview Show**.
Image 147: Above photo: **Inside of The Union Oyster House** in Boston. It is the restaurant of one of the nominated Chefs.

Image 138A and Image 138: **USS Midway Aircraft Carrier Museum and entrance sign in San Diego, California**

Image 137 and Image 137A: Above and Below **Inside Midway Museum.** I wrote, arranged and performed the music and sound effects for the Museum exhibits.

Image 139: Above: **Yuma State Prison**. Most haunted prison in the U.S.

Image 140: Below: **Lutes Casino** in Yuma Arizona. Eclectic memorabilia all over the place, and yes, we did look under the apron!

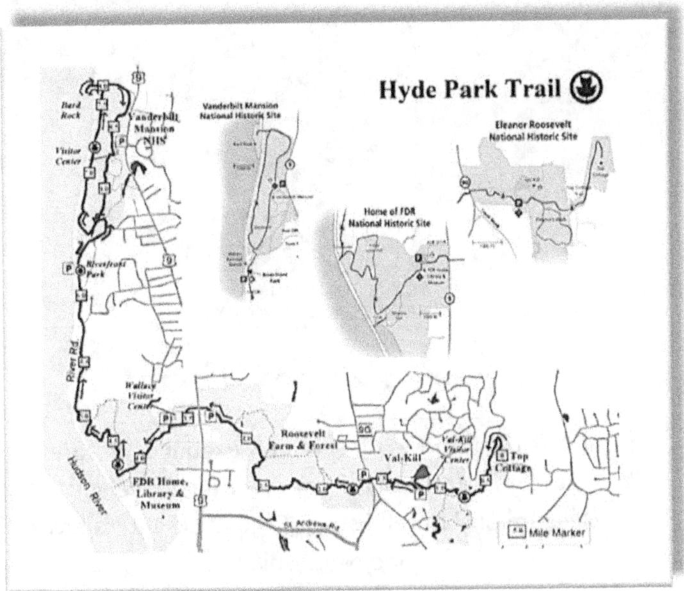

Image 141: Above: **Hyde Park Trail Map**. I recorded the audio tours for three museum sites on the Hyde Park Trail including The Franklin D. Roosevelt Mansion, Eleanor Roosevelt's retreat called Val-Kill and the Vanderbilt Mansion.

Image 142: Below: **Inside the Franklin D. Roosevelt Mansion.**

Image 143: Above: **Cleveland Museum of Natural History,** Wrote all the songs for the Cleveland Museum of Natural History, Ohio Rocks interactive Geology Display.

Image 144: and Image 145: Below: **Wrote Music for and Aspen Dental and Sterling-Signet Jewelers.**

25
BANDS

全全全

I don't know where the years have gone. Time seems to be just flying by. I have been busy engineering, writing original music and doing voice overs. Just busy moving forward while experiencing and enjoying what comes next. Then all of a sudden, it's 2011 and reality hits me, and hits me hard. A good friend and former band member Craig Balzer from American Noise died from cancer. It was devastating. In my mind he will always be the young healthy, good looking lead singer from American Noise. I felt like a piece of me died too. Life's mortality was now front and center.

Music has always been a safe place for me and a way to work through things during tough times. So, I knew what I had to do. I needed the camaraderie and fellowship of playing with a band.

I called my friend Jerry Zsigo. I knew he was playing in a band called Dr. Mo. The band did not have a keyboardist. He said it would be great to have me play with them but it wasn't his band. He gave me Monica Robins number. I had never met Monica. I only knew her as the

Senior Health Correspondent and Multi-Media Journalist from WKYC Cleveland television. I felt a little intimidated but I did call her. She was so gracious. She said she knew who I was and I absolutely could come and play with them. So, I did.

When I started to think about it, I realized that I hadn't played with a band live on stage since 1992 and it was now 2011. Jumping in to play with Monica's band was going to be interesting, but I knew I needed to do it.

I started to think that maybe I had been neglecting an important part of my life. Playing out live had been so much a part of me since I was young. How did I let this happen? But I couldn't worry about that now. I just needed to focus on playing my best with Monica's band.

Although I hadn't been playing out live, I still had been playing all the instrumental parts of the music I had been writing for my clients. So, my fingers were still nimble and my brain as always was in a musical mode. I had up-to-date keyboards and the microphones that I used in my studio. I just had to pull out an old monitor and stand and make sure I had all the correct cables. Before I knew it, I was ready to go.

It was a fantastic gig, just what I needed. I must have done a good job because Monica and Deke, her kilt wearing significant other who plays the drums, asked if I was interested in becoming their permanent keyboard player in their rock band the Whiskey Kings. I said, "Yes." I now had a regular gig playing with a band live on stage. I knew that this was the part of me I had been missing.

The Whiskey Kings played mostly bigger venues and the one I really enjoyed was Lock 3 in downtown Akron. It has entertained more than four million visitors and hosted the first Rock the Lock concert.

Playing live on stage now was much different than when I played with Eric Carmen on tour. The big difference was now there is no road crew. That means we set up everything ourselves and if something goes wrong, we have to fix it.

Once when our set up time was very tight, I was rushing and trying to set up my keyboard stand. It was totally jammed and no matter what I tried it wouldn't open. I played two keyboards at the time, so the stand was a heavy-duty model that was precisely set up to my requirements. I had no other option; I needed that keyboard stand. I borrowed a screwdriver from the venue sound crew and went to work. I totally dismantled that stand and reconstructed it piece by piece, screw by screw. Timewise it was close, but it got done and we started on time. I now pack a screwdriver kit in with my gear. Live and learn.

***

We also played for the yearly Cancer Walk in Wade Park, where so many cancer survivors would light a candle and walk in support of cancer research. It really touched my heart seeing so many survivors, but I had no idea of the real-life implications. It may even had been some foreshadowing for me, because in 2013 I became a cancer survivor myself.

I had played with Monica and Deke for about three years; and then as often happens life got in the way. It was the end of the year 2012 and all through 2013. Janet's and my health and well-being became a nightmare. We tried to be positive by saying, "We're just getting all the bad out at one time," but it was rough going.

Janet had three major surgeries and even went non-responsive twice during the last one. On the day she got home from the hospital her mother, who had lived with us for 12 years died.

On top of everything else, I got pancreatic cancer and was going through treatments for over a year. I thank God every day as well as my Oncologist Dr. O'Brien because everything worked out. I am now a cancer survivor. If I give any advice, it's to know your own body so you can identify small but persistent changes. Early detection is the key to surviving. OK, I will stop preaching now.

***

It took a while, almost two years but life finally got back to normal. I decided it was time to play out again. I played a duo with Jeff Varga. He played guitar and I was on keys. It was a great gig. We had a great back and forth between song that was perfect comic relief. It was a big hit. Janet called it the Jeff and George show. We were getting popular and it would have been fun to continue. Playing out two or three nights a week and balancing my advertising clients was difficult. More importantly, it wasn't fair to Jeff if I had to say no to a gig because of my clients. It just wasn't working.

***

As an alternative, here and there I started to fill in for friends with different bands. I would play keyboards or bass guitar. No rehearsals, no set lists just show up and play. It was fun and it certainly kept me on my toes. It led to some very interesting experiences.

Once many years ago, Sammy Free got a gig playing at a private campground. Sammy Free was on bass guitar, Sam Romano played drums and I was on keyboards, and as I remember it Cy Sulak was on guitar. We really didn't know much about the gig. We were just given the time and place and we all drove in our own cars. Janet decided to come with me and since it was such a long drive it was great to have the company.

As we turned into the campground, I was driving slowly on the dirt road. Looking for anyone from the band.

Suddenly I hear Janet say in a somewhat astonished tone, "Look, all the people over there have no clothes on!"

Then continuing on we noticed that almost everyone was naked. You guessed it. It is just what you are thinking. It was a nudist party. I couldn't have been more surprised.

I had no problem with playing for them, but I had one very important question, "Do they expect the band to be nude also?"

I was sure of one thing, that was never going to happen at least not with me. We played the gig fully clothed and actually had a great time.

During the break we saw that the nudists had built a large bonfire. The guys who were still nude took turns jumping over it. Didn't look like fun to me but everyone cheered and drank a toast with each jump. We were never going to jump the flames, but we did drink and cheer.

This whole experience was the first time that Janet and Sam Romano had met. To this day, every time Janet sees Sam she reminds him of that special gig long ago.

***

After a while, I thought about playing regularly with a band again. I had met Priscilla Zietlow and Mike Bender. They had a duo at local bars. Priscilla had a dynamite voice and I knew she would be a great lead for a full band. I will always remember what Mike said to me when we were talking about me playing the keyboards.

He said, "I didn't even know you played keys." That just goes to show, I had been away from playing on stage too long.

We formed a band called the Jam Machine. I enlisted Don Krueger for drums who was my former roommate from the Eric Carmen tours. Scott Emerson was on bass. Mike played guitar and Priscilla sang. Don, Scott and I created a strong rhythm section. Priscilla sang most of the songs while Mike played guitar and also sang.

Mike and Priscilla were able to form different configurations of the band to meet venue needs, a duo, trio, quartet or full band. This was great for Mike and Priscilla; they were always working. But it did make it hard for everyone else if they weren't playing the gig. This was especially hard if it was that band members sole income.

***

After a few great years with the Jam Machine, my musical wanderlust struck again; but what to do? As always opportunity provided the answer.

My Old friend Ed Sarley had been playing with a group called the Geeze Cats for nineteen years. He also played summers at Put-In-Bay with Bob Gatewood. If that wasn't enough, he also had his own band, Buzzy J and the Verbs, that filled in any open dates! As we were both not getting any younger, Ed decided to quit the Geeze Cats and his summer gig at Put-In-Bay and join me in a duo. We called ourselves, Those Guys.

We did some careful planning on what we would do. I had a synthesizer/workstation that allowed me to split the keyboard. I could play bass with my left hand and with my right hand I could play piano, organ or whatever was needed. This did work, but it was not the best answer to what we wanted to present. I didn't think the overall sound was strong enough, and playing bass with one hand threw off my ability to really play piano as I should!

We decided to try backing tracks. What we found were sites that allowed us to remix songs. We could take out any keyboard, guitar or vocals. We could then add any other instrumentation we wanted. This would give us the opportunity to play live as if we were with a full band.

And of course, I went one step further and created my own backing tracks, where we would sing the harmonies and I would record them myself. It was still Ed and I playing and singing live, just with my recorded backing tracks.

We then concerned ourselves with how to amplify our live sound. We knew we needed a decent sound system. We had seen groups using a Bose system for their PA. This system had a great overall sound, but louder! It consisted of a tall six-and-a-half-foot tube. This towering tube had 32 two-inch speakers directed in multiple directions and a sub-woofer with dual ten-inch speakers. The sound was able to be thrown toward the back of the room with almost the same intensity as in the front without a great deal of volume. How great for restaurant applications! When not using it at an extreme volume you can actually place the unit behind you without feedback. To our great relief, we don't have to drag a monitor system to the gigs.

Now we had to decide on our music choices. Because restaurants would be part of our venues, we had to withhold on playing loud rock music. Keeping this in mind we were able to find a variety of songs popular in the 60's, 70's, 80's, and 90's. Songs that the audience has probably heard and could sing along to. We learned a few slow songs, but only play them when requested. We also added some pop country tunes that the audience really liked.

I uploaded the audio and lyrics to my iPad. It allowed us to play the backing tracks and it gave us cheat sheets for the lyrics while on stage. Heaven knows we are not getting any younger and forgetting lyrics does happen.

In the beginning we didn't use a lot of backing tracks. Some naysayers didn't think it was acceptable. But as time went on, we realized that we were there to entertain. We needed to put our best foot forward and present the best show. The rest is history.

Going into the studio and recording a double track of some lead vocals to make them sound thicker worked out well. It really enhanced our end product. Using our own tracks allowed us to add Chicago songs with horns as well as other songs with big harmony parts. In the big picture, just like at any concert we are there to entertain. Our audiences love our show so we must be doing something right.

***

Playing with my longtime friend makes going to work a pleasure. And just like any other band we have had some unique experiences playing together.

One night while playing at a yacht club, a very nice and well to do gentleman kept putting in $100.00 bills in our tip jar, totaling a thousand-dollars! We asked him if there was something we could play for him. He asked for Ed Sheeran's *Shape of You*. Definitely not our style but we learned it anyway and played it for him the next time we saw him. He loved it. We were not surprised that from then on, he always gave us at least a two-hundred-dollar tip each night we played.

***

On the other hand, some nights are just strange. We played at a function where there was a formal dinner event in the dining room and then when they were finished eating everyone had to move to the bar. To our surprise they had us set up in the dining room instead of the bar. We had to arrange our set so we played quietly all during dinner. We were so quiet that I heard Ed's singing louder live than coming through the PA! After they were done eating everyone but one table went into the bar. So, we played the rest of the night for that one group and for the servers clearing the tables.

We finally played our last song and were starting to pack things up. Three fairly intoxicated women strolled into the room from the bar and asked for the song *Brown Eyed Girl*. What I thought and what I said were two different things.

I thought, "Whoa, you want us to play that old standby that we have played a million times during our careers. And you ask us to play it NOW, when you couldn't even be bothered to come in and listen to us when we were playing. "Hell, NO we won't play it!"

But of course, I didn't say that. Instead with a sweet smile on my face and a slightly sarcastic voice I said, "That would be a $20 in the tip-jar song." They smiled back at me and casually turned and sauntered or rather stumbled back to the bar. Thank goodness!

***

Nowadays, outdoor venues have become quite popular during the summer months. Unfortunately, they are booked months prior to the gig date. We never know what the weather will be like. Bar owners are always hopeful that the weather will cooperate. They will book bands early in the season and go late into the fall. Unfortunately, that doesn't always work out well for the bands. Once we played a gig where by the end of the night it was fifty-two degrees and a cold chilling wind was blowing. Let me tell you how hard it is to play keyboards or a guitar under those conditions. We were the only ones outside for the last set. Still, we played on because we wanted to get paid.

The other issue with some outdoor venues is the chance of rain! Usually that can be predicted before we start playing and then there is no issue. But we played a gig where a cloudburst came out of nowhere. We were quickly able to get the equipment under table umbrellas. We were lucky that it kept the equipment from getting ruined but unfortunately our cases got really wet. When the sun came back out, we found a somewhat dry spot and continued to play, but our cases never did dry that night. So, I drove home with all the gear unpack in the back of my SUV. I now keep tarps close by, even on sunny days. Living next to Lake Erie you can never trust a clear sky!

***

Yacht clubs are always interesting to play at. The venues are usually outdoor and the weather is usually warm and sunny. The people love to party and drink. Their boats or should I say yachts are beautiful. Many of the members use them as their summer homes and that is how this story starts.

One of the members who stayed on his boat all summer was drinking and partying and had gone to his boat for a short nap. Hours past and people had started to miss him and they started looking for him. All kind of speculation was going around to his whereabouts. They even ask for him over the PA but to no avail. The next day we found out that they had found him in the water. He never made it to his boat. They are assuming he fell off the dock from having too much to drink. It is a sad and cautionary tale. It is hard not to think of it whenever I am playing a yacht club gig.

***

As of this writing Ed and I play on the average of twice a week. Our Fridays and Saturdays are usually booked but lately we have been doing some Mondays and Thursdays too. I was just reflecting on when Ed and I first started playing out together. It was just before COVID started. We had no idea what we were in for. Things have really taken off. I must admit, toting equipment is getting harder as I get older. Maybe we should hire a road crew. I tried to talk Janet into being my road crew but she said, "No way!" It was worth a try.

Image 149A: **Just Me playing at Eastland Inn**
A Those Guys gig.

Image 149: Above: **Jerry Zsigo** playing guitar.

Image 150: Below: **American Noise**: Gerry Moran, Bruce Balzer, Greg Holt, (**Center Craig Balzer, RIP My Friend,**) Tommy Rich, and Myself.

Image 151: Above: **The Whiskey Kings**, Ken Cali, Deke Kumler, Luther Smith. Me, Brian McDonald, and front center Monica Robins.

Image 152: Below: **Playing a large outdoor venue**

Image 153: Above: **3-member Jam Machine,** Me, Priscilla and Mike Binder,

Image 154: Below: **5-member Jam Machine.** Always had a shot just before starting Don Kruger, Me, Scott Emerson, Mike Binder and Pricilla

Image 155: Below: **Cy Sulak and Sammy Free.**

Image 156: Right: **Sam Romano.**
Image 157: Below: **Jeff Varga**.

Image 158: Above: **Those Guys on stage.**
Myself and Ed Sarley

Image 159: Below: **Ed Sarley and Me.**

Image 160: Above: **Those Guys Schedule.** All the signs have **Those Guys** name on them.

Image 161: Below: **Flyer for Those Guys.** I create our own funny posters each week for advertisement.

Image 162: Above: **Those Guys Flyer.** Everyone thinks we are brothers, so I took both our faces and fused them side-by-side into one for this advertisement.

Image 163: Below: **Ed Sarley and Myself.**

26
COVID

仝仝仝

I must say that COVID was definitely a life altering experience. Not just for me, but for the whole world. It changed the way everyone does just about everything. From the smallest activity to a massive group event, everyone had to adjust.

Of course, as fate would have it, Ed and I had just started playing out when COVID hit. It had an impact on us both musically and financially. We took gigs for a while wearing masks, except of course while on stage. We also tried to get mostly outside gigs. That worked for a short time and then things started to get worse. More and more restaurants were closing. It got to the point that there was a full quarantine mandated and all work stopped.

Good friends were coming down with COVID. Our friend Don Krueger was hospitalized for weeks and to this day still has repercussions from it. He even had to learn how to speak, walk and play drums all over again.

Some other musician friends were not so lucky and lost their battle to COVID. The world is less harmonic without them. They are missed but will always be with us in every note of music that is played.

I feel that during this time bar owners realized they don't need bands playing until two in the morning. In fact, now that the COVID mandate has been lifted most bars are voluntarily closing early anyway. Years ago, we would just be going out at this time to see if we could pick up a girl. Times have changed.

Bar and restaurant owners also seemed to feel that because of COVID everyone was so hungry for work that they didn't have to pay bands what they deserved. It's been a long road to run but only now do I feel that bars are finally paying a living wage. That is really important to musicians when it's their main source of income.

***

COVID didn't just affect availability of playing out, it also affected my home studio business. It became null and void. My business for the most part was geared to large corporate meetings and all that went away with COVID.

Even to this day more companies are doing video conferencing instead of in-house meetings. This is not just for health reasons but because they can save so much money. It's the new norm.

But as I have always said, if you hit a brick wall, side step and learn a new skill, or apply what you already know in a different way. That is exactly what we did.

Mostly, Janet and I survived on our retirement money with some additional help from her children's book sales, art sales and a few of my clients that still needed work done.

***

During this time Steve Spinner my client from Fitness Quest, brought me a fantastic project. It couldn't have come at a better time. It was an infomercial where I did the narrating, music and audio assembly for a dog training video. It was a huge success and it led to another infomercial later on.

Strangely enough, I happen to run into Don Sullivan, The Dog Father, in our local Walgreens parking lot. This is quite a coincidence because he actually lives in Canada. He just happened to be driving back home and stopped at this Walgreens. It wasn't hard to identify him, he had his company name Don Sullivan, The Dog Father written across the side of his van. Small world isn't it.

***

I also had a project come through from Greg Mueller of Mueller Design called The Disruptive Dozen Project. It was for The World Medical Innovation Forum, which brings together global leaders to address the latest opportunities and challenges in the healthcare investment landscape and technology. I must have done something right, because I have done the project every year since.

***

Another recording and assembly project that helped get us through those tough times was the Brotherhood of Locomotive Engineers. It was recording and assembly work, and in spite of COVID, I was able to record two singers at separate times with a lot of extra precautions.

***

For the most part COVID put everyone in survival mode. Yet helping one another was first and foremost on all our minds. Everyone did whatever they could do.

Alex Bevan had a live hour-long show on the internet that helped to lift all of our spirits. As Alex says, "It's Music for what ails you." You can still find and enjoy his music live streaming online.

During COVID, every Thursday Janet created and posted a "Find and Count" image for kids. Not only was it fun and educational, but it helped to promote and sell her children's books and our art work. It was so popular that she even kept posting long after the quarantine mandate was lifted.

Image 164: Above: **Alex Bevan's Live Show, Music for What Ails You.**

Image 164A: Above: **Find and Count image. Janet created and posted one every Thursday during COVID.**

Image 165 Above: Logo for **The DogFather video.**
Image 166 Above**: Disruptive Dozen Show.**
I wrote music for both projects above.

Image 167: Below: Logo **Brotherhood of Locomotive Engineers.** Played and recorded music for them.

Image 168: Above **10 of the 12 books Janet illustrated and wrote.** Available on Amazon and Barnes and Noble. Or just type in **Janet Sipl books** in any search engine.

27

PAYING IT FORWARD

仝仝仝

At this stage of my life, sharing what I know and paying it forward gives me the greatest joy and personal satisfaction. It's the focus for my everyday motivation and goal setting. It is what makes my world-go-round.

***

I may have mentioned this before, but Janet was an elementary school teacher. Turns out that her principal Michael Kostyack was a big fan of American Noise. He and his wife Alaina went to see the band perform many times and even owned the album. One day Mike approached Janet and said, "My twelve-year-old daughter Georgia loves to sing, and I was wondering if there was anything George could do for her." I agreed to listen to her sing, so he brought her to the studio.

She was quite shy and cute as a button. I decided to make her feel comfortable in the studio setting by having her sing for me like she sings when she is at home. I had her choose her favorite song. I found a karaoke track and she sang her heart out. I must admit the beginning was a little rough, but she did have a sweet voice and I thought for sure we could make some great strides with a little training. I decided to give her some mentoring help. No formal lessons, no pay, just paying it forward like those who had helped me in the past. Besides, her father would always bring a great bottle of wine with him whenever he brought her over for a session.

Over the years she steadily improved. We talked about controlling her breathing and focusing on hitting high notes without screaming. She was like a sponge. She listened and applied everything and kept getting better and better.

And then she got a guitar and asked if I could give her guitar lessons. Unfortunately, I am not comfortable enough to teach guitar so I recommended someone who was a seasoned guitar teacher. Once she learned some basic chords, she began writing her own material. I was amazed. Her songs were really good.

She began performing at local fair type venues. I went to see her and was quite proud of what she had accomplished! Her Grandfather, who had purchased the beautiful Fender guitar for her was also there. He was quite the support group and really wanted her to become successful. He pulled me aside looked me in the eyes and said in no uncertain terms, "You *will* make her a star." I knew he loved her very much but I am not so sure he understood what the chances were and what it would take. My focus was to give her the tools to be the best singer songwriter that she could be.

Then, things took a disheartening turn. With her guitar teacher and visions of stardom, Georgia got busy with her new endeavors. I guess she outgrew me because I was now totally out of the picture. Her guitar teacher put together a band and an album's worth of material. He packed up Georgia and her Granddad and off to Nashville they went to record and make a video.

Being totally left out of the loop at this point I only found out later that all did not end up well. The guitar teacher who had played hard rock and heavy metal style music in his career had put together a band that didn't have a country background. I found that strange because most everything Georgia wrote was country. I guess tempers flared, a lot of money was spent and Georgia did not become the star that Grandpa wanted.

I was heartbroken. I had nurtured and helped to develop her voice and she was becoming a promising singer and songwriter. So, when I talked to Georgia, I offered her my arranging talent and my studio to record her originals. I would be happy to do that, and just like before at no cost to her. I couldn't let those great songs just die. She agreed and we began working together.

Georgia would come over with a new song. I would record her singing and playing the guitar and then she would let me at it!

OK, here comes the techy stuff, I would take the track and compress and stretch it into a solid metronomic beat. This was so that when I added a drum track, it wouldn't speed up and slow down.

As there was no budget the tracks were entirely created by me in the studio. I had some great instrument samples but purchased a plugin that would emulate a banjo, steel guitar and give me some other great acoustic guitar sounds.

Georgia would then come in and sing the final lead vocals and harmonies to the fully orchestrated version of her song that I created. I would then mix it.

During COVID the process changed. One of the things that I noticed was when I was talking to someone on my Bluetooth in the car and they were on their iPhone it sounded so clear. It made me wonder if the microphones in an iPhone were actually fairly decent! So, I figured I'd give it a try!

I asked Georgia to record her voice and guitar in her clothes closet so that it deadened the room ambiance and didn't sound too hollow. For what it was, the results were astounding. It really sounded pretty good.

I would do an arrangement and send her an mp3 of the instrumental. I asked her to load that mp3 into her iPad and attach headphones. Then take her iPad and wearing the headphones go into the closet. I told her to put her iPhone on a table or something sturdy and sing into it as she followed the mp3 on her iPad.

She then proceeded to send me the files with just her vocals. I had her do three or four takes. This gave me the option to steal a note or phrase if needed. I then mixed the piece. I played it for a few of my friends who were engineers without telling them how I did it. I wanted an honest critique. It passed with flying colors!

Georgia still plays out occasionally but hasn't been in to record for a while. She's now a married woman to Mitch who was her High School sweetheart. I made sure to meet him and give my OK. All kidding aside, Mitch is a fantastic person. She couldn't have picked a better life partner.

Working with her was some of the most rewarding work I've done in my career. She allowed me complete production control with her songs, never a complaint or change. She always gave me a big smile and said she loved them! It was a real pleasure taking this "diamond in the rough" and making great music. Her songwriting excelled to be totally legitimate pieces of art. Her vocal is strong, clean and on pitch. I am indeed quite proud!

•••

Parents will often tell me about their child, who has some musical talent. They want my "honest" opinion, or for me to help in some way. But not all of them want the truth. It can become very tricky, especially if the child is not that good. They may be good in terms of the other kids in their school or church; but to succeed in the Music business it is a whole different story.

Here is a perfect example. Once a neighbor asked me to speak to their son. He came to see me because his mother wanted him to be a Music major in college. I felt she wanted me to share what great opportunities there are in the music business. Unfortunately, this is just not reality. The options of becoming a star were minimal, and the other options with his instrument of choice were limited.

But none of this mattered to him because he didn't even want to play music as a career. So, I asked him what he did like. His whole demeanor changed. He said he loved video and cameras, filming and such. We went on to have an illuminating discussion about different options for careers in business that would involve working with what he loved to do. When he left, he felt confident that he was on the right track in choosing a non-musical major. Mom was not in agreement and she let me know it.

Anyway, the boy finished college with a Film and Media Arts degree. He was ecstatic and now was looking for work. His mom decided to give me another call. And with a snide tone in her voice she said, "Well, now you can find him a job. You got him into this career."

Whoa, that is not at all how it happened. But I liked the kid and I did have a few contacts I could tap for him. So, I did.

I called my buddy Pat Murray who in his career had directed over 2,500 major league baseball games and over 500 Cleveland Cavaliers games for various TV stations. He had over 16 Emmy's to his name. I figured if anyone could help, Pat could.

I told Pat that I had a good Catholic Irish boy who just graduated Cleveland State with a degree from the school of Film and Media Arts. His main goal was to work as a cameraman for sporting events. Pat chuckled and said to send him to his office. His exact words were, "I'll take care of him!"

He's been doing camera work for sporting events for over 10 years now. He gets to travel all over the United States and loves his job! We have stayed in contact over the years. We even went to his wedding with Pat Murray. I'm glad it all worked out.

***

One ongoing experience I find very rewarding is being asked to speak to the audio/video students at both Polaris/Berea Midpark, and The Cuyahoga Valley Career Center. I focus on the techniques involved in recording and mixing. During class I have the students actually edit voiceover tracks that I have recorded.

They start out thinking this diminutive task is beneath them. But soon they are astonished when the reality of actually listening, hearing and editing the tempo of human speech catches up to them. Do they know how long a pause is between sentences; or if you cut out the breath, do you still leave a space? Actually, they never thought of it. All the editing knowledge and techniques I share are fundamental constants that will serve them well in their audio career. I also talk about miking instruments like drums, guitars and even vocals. I also share some special tips and tricks I have learned over the years.

It is always amazing to see how the students get quite receptive to new information when they realize how much they still have to learn. This old guy still has a trick or two up his sleeve!

***

One more thing before I forget. This came as a total surprise to me. I received an award from the City of Seven Hills for my music and music production work. It recognizes my achievements, as well as my community service of paying it forward. A photo plaque is now hanging on a wall in Seven Hills City Hall as a member of their Hall of Fame!

Having grown up in Seven Hills this honor was very special to me. It was an amazing surprise! I must give thanks to the Kostyack family, especially Alaina, for nominating me!

Image 169A: **Photo Plaque from Seven Hills Hall of Fame.**

Image 169: Above: **One of Georgia's Albums.**

Image 170: Below: **Georgia OHara (Kostyack) and myself.**

Image 171: Above: **Georgia Kostyack** when I first started working with her.

Image 172: Below: **Georgia Kostyack with her guitar.**

Image 173: Above: **Georgia Kostyack** on Detroit Tiger's jumbotron singing The National Anthem live.

Image 174: Below: **The Kostyack Family**. Daughters Arlene and Maria, Dad Michael, Daughter Georgia, Mom Alaina. Charcoal sketch by Janet Sipl.

28
SAVED THE BEST FOR LAST

仝仝仝

Each person I have mentioned below deserves their own chapter in this book. They have helped me, influenced me or even at times had to kick me in the butt. But most importantly, they have all been my friends. Thank you all for being a part of my life.

***

Alex Bevin: We had no formal introduction. Just knowing each other's reputation pulled us together. Whenever I'm not playing and he is, Janet and I try to make it! He is my wife's favorite and she has great taste.

Alex is a modern-day troubadour, a great singer, songwriter and storyteller. His acoustic guitar playing is unsurpassed. When Alex picks up his guitar and starts to play and sing it's nostalgic. Moments like that cannot be replicated.

On a side note, his looper abilities that he does so well have often baffled this old audio guy! Keep looping my friend. You are one in a million.

***

Ann Thompson: For many years Ann's *After the Gig* was a way to let people know who's playing where in the Cleveland area! She knows her rock and roll and is a great supporter of local talent.

Nowadays we only seem to see Ann on Christmas. She throws one hell of a party with her husband John! Ann could have been a chef!

***

Bill March: Bill is so talented and easy to get along with that he plays bass with many different bands. So many that I can't even list them! He is not only a phenomenal bass player but he plays the acoustic guitar, sings, and is a song writer. Those are just some of his many talents.

I have had the pleasure of not only playing with Bill, but I have done some producing, arranging, and recording of his original songs. Bill is multi-talented and a gentleman through and through. Who can ask for more?

***

Billy Sullivan: I have known Billy forever. I think the first time we met was back when I engineered for his band Club WOW. I have mentioned him a few times in the book. He is my go-to guy. The singer of the *IX Indoor Amusement Park* jingle, guitar player for numerous corporate pieces I wrote, guitar player for Herman Hermits. The list goes on and on. But I also wanted to mention the duo he has with Rich Spina, called Spina/Sullivan when he is not on the road with Herman Hermits.

Billy is truly talented and successful in his own right, but with his beautiful wife Debbie they are a couple to admire. She is the heart and soul of his family. We love you both.

***

Brian Gary Varga: The "Big Wise"! So aptly named by drummer Michael McBride! One of the most important jobs of any tour which is so often overlooked is that of the road crew. Hard work, lack of sleep, an occasional meal and no standing ovation at the end of the night! Who could ask for more!

"Wise" was our stage manager for the Eric Carmen band! I depended on him, and he never disappointed!

***

Cy Sulak: With guitar slung low like a western gunman, Cy can shoot out a lead for any song imaginable. See what I did there? I don't care who you are, that was funny!

For years he conducted the Sly Fox Jam on Wednesday nights and hosted the Refuse No Song Challenge. He never missed a beat. He really knows and can play anything rock and roll.

Cy and I also played together in a group consisting of John Salamon on keys, GG Greg on drums, Cy on guitar and I played bass. We were playing a gig at Peak and Peak ski resort in New York. Shortly before we were to start, we found out that John had broken and splintered his leg skiing that day. John went to the hospital and the gig was canceled. Since we weren't playing, the rest of us decided to stay and drink for the whole weekend. Sorry to say it was a very long recovery for John; and our hangovers took a while as well!

On an important side note: I am pleased to say that Cy has now been sober for over 18 years! Couldn't be prouder!!!!! Love ya man!

***

Don and Andrea Krueger: I have mentioned Don many times in the book. But I have to mention him again. He is someone who I've played in more bands with than anyone else. And believe it or not, we're still friends!

He is a dynamic drummer and a great tour partner on the road, but most of all he has a heart full of goodness. You couldn't ask for a more loyal friend.

He really gave everyone a scare during COVID. But as always with Andrea's help (his beautiful wife), Donny came out a winner. I knew 14 years ago when Don married Andrea that he had a partner for life! They are made for each other. Love you both!

***

Eddie Tomecko Owner of Audio-VideoWorks: Eddie and I got together a few years back as he was producing his yearly Christmas album using local talent. The proceeds went to Akron General Children's Hospital. Eddie needed me for string arrangements, keyboards, and occasionally to help with getting vocals together. Janet did the CD covers for all the albums.

I also once told Eddie about this great band I had seen with this dynamite female lead singer. I guess he thought so too, they married this year! Congratulations Marysa and Eddie. You are made for each other.

***

Eric Carmen: I believe Eric is one the finest popular songwriters of our time. His classical training has served him well.

What a great opportunity it was to be able to work with him. It was the learning experience of a life time. I wouldn't have missed it for the world! Thank you, Eric!

***

Jay Millward and John Milllward: John is the drummer for Northern Lights. A band I recorded at After Dark in the early 80's and still play the occasional gig with to this day. John is always ready to help and does not know the phrase, "No, I can't." He also has a wife Sue who is beautiful and never ages. Janet wants her secret.

Anyway, when Scott the lead guitar player for the Northern Lights band moved to Florida, John recommended his nephew Jay to fill in. Oh shit, it's a family member. This should be good! Well, it was absolutely great! Jay was outstanding. He even filled in with Monica Robins band the Whiskey Kings. Besides being a great guitar player Jay rides a Harley! Who could ask for more?

***

Jim and Kathy Bacha: Another couple where it's been so long I don't remember exactly where we met. Kathy worked upstairs from the Agora and Jim was playing in one of his many bands. It was a given they had to get together.

Jim now plays bass for Monica Robins country band, the Ninja Cowboys. For many years he was one of the mainstays for the Wednesday Jam at the Sly Fox with Cy Sulak. Like Cy he would never balk at a song request and then play it like he rehearsed it the night before! He has talent galore. He and Kathy are the best of the best. Great looking couple!

***

Jimmy Clark: Jimmy has the ability to make a drum kit shake with fear, as if it knew of the beating it was about to get! Jimmy is Metallica's drum tech and actually fills in when Lars can't make the gig.

A few years back Janet and I saw Jimmy at a club wearing this outrageous Metallica leather jacket! Janet made a point of saying how much she liked it. Jimmy said, "I'll get you one." It was great for him to offer but we thought it was just a nicety and had forgotten about it. Jimmy has much more important things on his mind then getting Janet a coat.

Anyway, when we played together at Frank Amato's Autism Awareness Christmas Show, Jimmy walks in backstage with a large package. He was looking for Janet and I then remembered about the jacket. I just looked at him and said, "No way!" Janet held back the tears as she saw this gorgeous coat! Friends forever! We love you, Jimmy. But now I think Janet loves you just a little more than me. Can't image why!

***

Jim Stamper and Mary: Yes, he was our first drummer in SRO. But in later years he and his wife Mary became famous when they ran their family-owned bar in Lakewood called the Tam 'O Shanter. Jim and Mary later created "Stampers" bar in Fairview Park which was another musician's bar.

The Tam was a very popular bar and became famous for the Jam at the Tam. If you were anybody in rock and roll, you played at the Tam. Another friend Drew Losch videoed the Jams and saved them for posterity. These were true jams as there was rarely a formed band playing. It was then I first saw the 16-year-old sax player, Tony Koussa, perform. Later Tony became a phenom of the guitar and keys as well! The Tam was a great place to be noticed.

In an interview Tom Hanks was talking about his time with the Great Lakes Shakespearian group in Ohio. He said, "The Tam was his favorite place to hang out!" For me too! To this day, the Tam is still one of my favorite places I have played! Thanks Jimmy and Mary for being a part of my life.

***

Krista and Eric Rasmussen are two of my biggest supporters. They always come to see me play. Krista is a talented artist in her own right, yet she took the time to proof my book. She is all about giving and is relentless about working for the Make a Wish Foundation.

Her husband Eric is always right there to give a hand when it is time to load up after a gig. He is the best road crew I could ever ask for. I wish I could con him into helping every gig but he is too smart for that. I always look forward to our Tuesdays and Thursdays out, drinking with Jeremy and the gang.

***

Lisa Caito: A tremendous female singer. Played in a group with Cy called Victory Highway, a country band called The Caliber Band, and a duo called Hit List with Dino Merlini. Dino is the man of a thousand voices! You ask for a song and you get it in the original singer's voice!

Lisa is a dream to work with in the studio. She is always spot on. She has a heart of gold and even recorded the song *Killing the Blues* for Janet's birthday. I can't tell you how often Janet plays it, over and over again.

***

Lou LaGuardia and Jennifer: Lou went off to California and came back a few years later with his beautiful wife Jennifer! The four of us: Janet, Jennifer, Lou, and myself struck up a great relationship. The girls are two peas in a pod. I think Lou and I are in trouble.

We go to hear Lou sing, and he returns the favor! Lou and Jennifer are our special wine buddies. They really know their stuff! And, they throw tremendous get-togethers. We are glad to have them as friends.

***

Lynn Jerrel: I've known Lynn from back in the American Noise days when she dated Craig Balzer. Lynn had been the lead singer in a band called Raisin Cane that was a very popular lounge band! I have used her talents on many a session. She even worked on the Ohio Rocks project for me. Needless to say, she is a talented singer!

***

Mark Thomsen: My dear friend Mark died of aids back when it was a death sentence. He was one of the greatest tenors I'd ever worked with. I had never worked with a gay man before so I was in need of an education! I told Mark, "I really love working with you, but you know I would never want you to hit on me!" His reply was perfect and taught me a lot! "What's makes you think you're my type?" RIP, my friend. We miss you!

***

Michael and Doug: Michael purchased a photo of Janet's at Perk-Cup, the coffee shop where we sell our photos. It wasn't quite lying flat in the frame and he wondered if we could fix it. I said, "Sure!" Michael came over, I fixed the photo and the rest is history!

I found out Michael was a chef and taught culinary arts and I love to cook! We then met Doug his partner, who is a master gardener and their three King Charles Cavalier dogs. The four of us and our five dogs make a great team. The dogs especially love it.

***

Monica Robins and Deke Kumler: I mentioned them earlier but it bears mentioning them again. I played in their band Whiskey Kings for a number of years and it was a really special time. Monica's voice is HOT! Country, blues, soul absolutely anything she nails.

Deke is a great drummer, and my wife thought the kilts he wore were a statement maker, especially for a drummer. Monica has a heart of gold and is always doing something for someone. She is what makes this world go round. She is a role model that we all could learn from. Monica, you have our hearts!

***

Octavian and Maggie: Our great neighbors! A quick story. When they first moved in and I met Octavian for the first time he said to me, "I hope you don't mind, but I have a rock band and we practice in our garage." Of course, his garage faces our family room!

My reply was, "Cool, I'm a musician too! We should jam together!"

He was shocked! He said, "No, No … I meant that as a joke to shake you up!" I told him I wasn't joking! We've been great friends ever since!

***

Rich Spina: I mentioned Rich going back to recording him in Unknown Stranger, but our relationship didn't stop there. He and Billy Sullivan currently play for Peter Noone and Herman's Hermits. He has also backed up hundreds of pop artists from the 60's on up. Not only a vocalist, Rich also plays piano, bass, guitar, sax, and God knows what else.

For years he had a Jaguar that he absolutely loved. My wife also had the same model jag for years. And of course, we both loved our little dogs. Buddy his little pup, would come over and play in the backyard with my two westies when Rich had a session. RIP Buddy, we miss you.

***

Sam Romano: Yes, the same Sam of the infamous nudist party gig. Here is how we met. I was filling in as the "musician du jour" in a band called the Buzz Band. The lineup was never the same but it worked because we stuck to playing the standards that everyone knew.

Sam was playing drums on many occasions. He was a fantastic drummer. Then once while the band was on break, Sam asked if he could try my keys. I said, "Sure!" Well, he absolutely blew me away. Then on another break, I heard him playing guitar! I mean this man is amazing! He's also a great vocalist! Don't you just love talented people? I do

***

Sammy Free: Yes, this is the other Sammy from the infamous nudist party gig. This Sammy is a great bass player and I have played with him in many different bands over the years.

Just to refresh your memory on the nudist gig. Sammy Free once hired me for a gig at some outdoor event. Not much info, but the pay was good! It was really hidden away in a private park! I brought Janet along as company. As we pulled in, Janet says, "Look, these people are naked, and then adds many of them shouldn't be!" She was right! But the men's nude fire jumping contest was a high point of the evening! We got to cheer the jumpers and drink a toast for each jump.

Anyway, thanks for the gig, and for marrying that gorgeous wife of yours, Cindy. You are a very lucky man!

***

Stein (Bill) and Kathy Mesich: We don't remember exactly when we first met. Stein was a "Rowdy Roadie" at the Cleveland Agora. Kathy hung with the sound company, and since I played there that is probably where we all met.

How can I describe Stein? Well, once when Janet was cold, Stein literally gave her the shirt of his back! That's him through and through. He has a heart of gold and a work ethic that never quits. Kathy his wife is his soul mate. The four of us have been great friends for many years. But actually, we are really more like family. Just never play cards with Kathy!

***

Steven Kohn: Steve was Jim Brickman's arranger back in Jim's jingle writing days. Now Steve writes complex highbrow orchestra pieces which is way above my pay grade!

A cute story I have to share: The first time Janet and Steve met, he asked her, "So what instrument do you play?" To which Janet smiled and replied, "Sorry, I don't play an instrument." Then Steve went on to say, "Oh, so do you sing?" Jan again smiled sweetly and replied, "No, I don't sing either." Without another word being said, Steve just turned and looked at me. I wondered if he was thinking, "Why would I marry this girl, she is not musical in anyway?"

And yes, I did marry Janet anyway, even though she freely admits she has no musical talent. Steve says he doesn't even remember the situation. But it doesn't matter because Steve, Janet and I are all still friends.

***

Tommy Amato and Judi: I believe I first met Tommy in the early 80's when we both lived in Lakewood. He has always had the reputation of being a great drummer. He is a cancer survivor and has used his musical legacy to help others with cancer.

Tommy created and hosts, with the help of his beautiful and talented wife Judi, the Tommy Amato Rock Relief show. It's a fundraiser to benefit musicians and families who are dealing with cancer. I tip my hat to both of them. Their giving and generosity are noteworthy. You both make this world a better place. Side note, Janet loves Judi's decorating. She really has a special touch!

***

Westside Steve Simmons: Steve is a true troubadour in every sense of the word. He is an amazing singer and songwriter. I've recorded that great voice for his early band Easy Street, and I have used him on commercials. One of my favorites is when I recorded him singing Christmas carols! Such great power in that voice! Janet says, "His voice can give you goosebumps."

In the hot summer months, you can find him at Put-In-Bay or in Key West, but always under an umbrella so he won't burn! Stay shaded my talented friend. You are one of a kind. Thanks for touching my life.

***

Weasel Strychnine: Yes, it is his real name on his driver's license. A name not easy to forget. Because of his hustle, this hard-working guy earned the reputation of being the "go to" guy for any sort of media needs! If you are a touring band looking for a particular instrument, or a film crew needing a particular car, Weasel was the one you would call.

Weasel and I are friends, he is a true gentleman and he is one of my wife's favorite people. He always makes her smile! Couldn't ask for more! Oh, and if I need a bad joke, he is definitely the one to call!

***

Neil Zaza is an amazing guitarist and he is known for his instrumental rock compositions. He tours all over the world mesmerizing his audiences. His dynamic stage presence and smile are always part of the show. His concerts are not to be missed.

I was honored to play on one of his albums, and I worked with him and his talented wife Theresa on her Christmas Show. I am blown away by his talent. He is a true artist of his craft.

***

Mr. Zonneville who is better known as Charlie Wiener has been a big help in formatting this book. He is always willing to help in any way he can. But I would be remiss if I didn't also mention that he is an all-around super talented dude. He is not only a talented musician, but he is also an accomplished writer having authored nine books. One of our favorite sides of Charlie is his comedic persona. He may be retired from touring stand-up on stage, but we get to continue to enjoy his natural inner funny all the time. Both Janet and I are proud to call him our friend. Love you, man!

29

ALL IN THE FAMILY

全全全

This next group of people are significant in a special way. They are my family by birth and by marriage. They have supported, encouraged and have made me laugh. They accepted me for who I am and have made me feel special. Whether I had long hair and a beard or had short hair and corporate clients, I was respected, accepted and made to feel like a valued part of the family. Some have passed away but their impact on my life will never be forgotten.

I have written many pages on my parents and the impact they have had on my life. Their drive and work ethic, along with their capacity to dream a dream and keep working until you attain it, all came from them. I thank them for that.

***

My brother Mike, who was in the Forced Labor Camp with my mother and sister, was a powerful influence in my life. As a child he had polio and had to wear leg braces and walk with a cane, but that never stopped him from enjoying life. His courage, determination and work ethic were inspirational.

He lived in California and was very successful with his financial endeavors. He had a beautiful home on the top of a mountain with a unique in-ground swimming pool and hot tub build in the backyard. When American Noise was recording in California, Mike had the whole band over for a day in the pool. He was an integral part of my life's journey and one of my biggest fans. Many of my character traits are a reflection of him. I can see these same attributes in his son Brent and his daughter Michelle.

He was into off-road motorcycling and had his own plane. Tragically, it was this very activity that took his life. He died piloting his own plane when flying to Mexico. Before the Mexican police arrived, the locals had stripped everything off the plane. They even took the leg braces he was wearing. RIP brother, I miss you.

***

My sister Ann is a story all her own. Coming from the Gakowa Forced Labor Camp in Yugoslavia, to then having to move to America, she was still able to beat all the odds. Ann went on to own two casinos, the Queen of Hearts and the Nevada Hotel in downtown Las Vegas. Both casinos had full gaming licenses. She was one of the first women in Nevada to ever have obtained a full gaming license. Again, Ann beat all the odds.

Her resilience and drive are all part of the inherent characteristics that make our family achieve their goals. She sets her mind to do something and she does it. She can be a force to be reckoned with and she has passed these traits on to her daughter Bridget and beautiful granddaughter Aspen.

When I had cut my fingers off and was going through recovery my sister drove to Ohio to visit me and bring me some joy. By joy I mean a large garbage bag of homegrown joy. It really helped relieve the pain.

Speaking of fingers, more than once a severed finger has been found in her casino hotel rooms. WOW, scenes from a Mafia movie just popped into my head. But we will never really know the whole story of how the fingers got there, and I don't think I really want to know.

***

I would be remiss if I did not mention this next group of people. They are all from Janet's side of the family, but because of their openness and support we are actually just one large extended family!

Janet's son Alan and our granddaughter Savannah Madison are on the top of this list. Alan and I have a great relationship. I love the fact that he will call and ask me some dumb trivia question that he can't answer. Yet, when it comes to finance, he is definitely the one I call. He is a financial wizard. He travels the world with his daughter Savannah. She plays World Cup Soccer and he never misses a game. Now in college, Savannah has both a soccer and academic scholarship at Virginia Tech. We are very proud of them both.

At first, with me having long hair and being a musician, I wasn't sure how everything was going to play out becoming Alan's stepfather. Well, my fears never materialized. In fact, many times it was Alan and I on the same wave length with Janet on a completely different channel. At least that is what she would say. One thing we all agree on though is Alan's girlfriend Stacey. She is constant in our lives and we are lucky to have her.

Our journey together has been full of adventure, laughter and growth. Thanks for letting me be your stepdad, and I love being Savannah's grandfather. I am so proud of you both.

***

Janet's younger brother Greg Sifferlen and his wife Sherriah are a team made in heaven. They are always welcoming, fun and on the move. They now live in New Hampshire on a beautiful estate with his daughter Carys (she is Janet's clone), Cary's husband Jeff and their son Asher.

Greg is the perfect brother-in-law. I don't think we have ever had a disagreement. Everything just clicks in a good way. Greg knows his music and it's always fun to debate bands with him.

***

Al Sifferlen is Janet's older brother. He is a true hero. He is a Vietnam Vet who has been in a wheelchair since he came home from the war. He lives with his daughter Jacquie, her husband David and their 5 boys.

His wife, Lynn died suddenly a few years ago and it left a hole is everyone's heart. But just as always, Al kept moving forward. I have always looked at him and been so impressed by his fortitude. He has passed these same traits on to his daughter Jacquie. Her patience and love are the core of their family.

Al never fails to tell me how proud he is of anything I accomplish. I am blessed to be in the same family with him.

***

Finally, the two people I had the most contact with and who had the most impact on my life, Janet's dad and mom, Albert and Dorothy Sifferlen.

Janet's dad was a first born American of German descent, just like me. He had a strength of character that I really admired. He was a tall, intelligent and an active silver haired retiree when I first met him. I was really worried when we went down to Florida to meet them. When I first walked in, I was in awe of her dad's presence. He firmly shook my hand and gave me a smile that reassured me. I knew then that everything was going to be just fine. We really clicked and became very close over the years.

He was very supportive and I often caught him bragging to others about me. That was really cool! When he passed away, I felt like I lost my own dad. He really had become such a positive force in my life.

***

Janet's mom came to live with us when her dad died. Dorothy was 84. She lived with us for 12 years until she passed away at the age of 96. I wasn't sure how it would work out, but it was actually great.

I had my studio at home so I was able to keep an eye on her during the day. Janet would be home from school before 4:00 most days and would take over. The way our home was set up, her mom had her own suite upstairs with her own kitchen, bath and a TV room. I put up cameras in all rooms so I could monitor and make sure she was safe while I was in the studio. She had an emergency button she could push if she needed me. It really worked out well.

Most of all I think it was her optimistic Irish attitude that made everything work. We would take her out to eat with us. I don't think she had ever been in a bar before she moved in with us. When she met our friends, she always showed interest in them and would make them feel special. Her Irish smile was always beaming through.

When I won my first *Emmy,* we called Janet's mom to share the news. I am not sure she knew exactly what the award was all about but you would have thought I had found the pot of gold at the end of the rainbow. She was so excited for me. This was her mom and I miss that a lot.

***

My journey has been filled with so many supportive people. Each person has had an impact on my life in a different way. I value each one of you. The world is a better place with you in it. Even though I may neglect to tell you, I am telling you now, thank you for being a part of my life.

Image 175A: Below: **My older brother Mike.** RIP Bro, I miss you every day.

Image 175B: Above: Our son **Alan Sabo and our granddaughter Savannah Madison Sabo.**

Image 175C: Below: **My sister Ann Sipl Meyers.**

30
RETIREMENT, I THINK NOT

全全全

When people ask, "Are you retired?" The answer is, "Yes and no." No, because Janet and I still create and sell our art. No, because I still play out with Ed Sarley in our band Those Guys about twice a week. No, because I still do audio engineering and writing music for a few clients.

But a big "Yes I am retired," because I now have the option of saying, "Sorry, I'm retired," when I don't want to do something. It's a great time to be alive!

Retirement means there is more personal creative time! Ever since High School, I've had an affinity for photography. I never wanted to be a photographer but enjoyed taking photos, creating memories and art. Then digital cameras and Photoshop arrived and it made a big difference to access, affordability and creativity. There was no limit to my imagination or what I could create. What a great time to be alive.

One day just before a trip to Atlanta Janet asked me to purchase a small digital camera for her. Of course, I loved the idea. I was excited that she was showing an interest in something we could do together. When we got home, she entered one of the photos she had taken into a local but very prestigious photo contest. She won the top award for her macro image of an orchid. That was it there was no stopping her now.

Since then, we have both taken classes, bought more equipment, and have a hobby that we enjoy together. Thirty-seven years later we are still doing it together. Yes, I mean our photography. We sell our work at a coffee shop in Berea, Perk Cup Café. We have around thirty images up at any given time. We do two shows a year in the Spring and Fall when we change everything out.

Janet has continued her study of Photoshop Artistry and takes classes online with an international art group that has students from all over the world. She has become quite the digital artist. Her artwork has been on the cover of *Living the Photo Artistic Life Magazine* including a five-page spread. She has completed four book covers for other authors and four CD covers for Christmas albums. But her most exciting achievement is that she has written and illustrated twelve children's books of her own. This allowed her to combine her knowledge of teaching and of Photoshop in a creative way. Her books sell on Amazon and at Barnes and Noble. Just type in Janet Sipl Books into any search engine and they will show up.

I also need to say a few special words about Janet. I made her write this exactly as I wrote it. In spite of all that I've have accomplished in my career, nothing is as significant as the love I have for her. I know I wouldn't be where I am today without her. But even if I had achieved it all, nothing would have been as sweet without her being there. She is my advisor, my confident, my biggest fan and most importantly my friend. As I always say, "She is my Rock while I Roll."

Image 175: Below: **Soaring Gull.** This is a photo I took of a seagull soaring in the sky, and I turned it into a large canvas. Since the book is in black and white you can't see the colors, but check out my site to see everything in color. https://www.flickr.com/photos/georgesipl/

Image 176: Above: **Tsunami,** I took this from Janet's hospital
room at University Hospital, Cleveland, Ohio.
**In the background, the Peter B. Lewis Building by Architect
Frank Gehry**
**In the foreground, Church of the Covenant. That is some
view, the old against the new.**
https://www.flickr.com/photos/georgesipl/

Image 177: Below: **The Cellist.** This is one of Janet's beautiful creations. If you stare are her bow hand you can almost see it move. She is a genius with photoshop. Check out her website to see everything in color. https://www.flickr.com/photos/janetsipl/

Credits:

All images in this book are part of George Sipl's Collection unless otherwise stated on these credit pages.

Image 2,
donauschwabenusa.org/3011_2A_children_orphanage_starve_to_death.JPG
Image 19
www.ignatius.edu/
Image 21
clevelandmemory.contentdm.oclc.org/digital/collection/heart/id/135/rec/2
Image 22
clevelandhistorical.org/files/fullsize/0f1d5d5790720712eb89df286788d766.jpg **Image 25**
3.bp.blogspot.com/-0SSBNz27t5k/Vg2VHM5LDel/AAAAAAAATew/MBmvtLVxxUE/s1600/75-march-21-Big-Dick-ad-
final.jpg
Image 32
upload.wikimedia.org/wikipedia/en/8/80/Eric_Carmen_%281975_Eric_Carmen_album_-_cover_art%29.jpg
Image 33
encrypted-tbn2.gstatic.com/images?q=tbn:ANd9GcRNTOvMGXVfb_PULXIFkZo7JH5Xtv4TpulhgTgaZHSrt6be3BER
Image 34
encrypted-tbn0.gstatic.com/images?q=tbn:ANd9GcSlN2_OdrB_8EAJj-
spl8jKNNjvuK8ThOMG8nazZTmHkZ2_W33ucM1Ls7f6VtYnTulYlsA&usqp=CAU
Image 35, Image 37, Image 38, Image 39 and Image 39
www.pinterest.com/pin/246220304598726545/
Image 41
Brian Gary Varga, Production Manager Archives.
Image 43
Brian Gary Varga, Production Manager Archives.
Image 44
Brian Gary Varga, Production Manager Archives
Image 46
Brian Gary Varga, Production Manager Archives.
Image 47
Brian Gary Varga, Production Manager Archives.
Image 48
m.media-amazon.com/images/I/71Aup88wARS._AC_UF1000,1000_QL80_.jpg
Image 49 and **Image 57**
Brian Gary Varga, Production Manager Archives.
Image 61
https://www.djtees.com/cdn/shop/articles/baxter.png?v=1503698375
Image 61A https://www.paramountmovies.com/uploads/movies/pretty-in-pink/pp-resize-prettyinpink-800x1200-
c.jpgand **Image 61B** Polly Novak Balzer
Image 76A
https://i.iheart.com/v3/catalog/artist/34155?ops=fit(720%2C720)
Image 78
i.ebayimg.com/images/g/eNQAAOSwhwtjUxOb/s-l1600.jpg
Image 79A
https://www.nin.wiki/images/thumb/7/7e/Reznorexoticbirds.jpg/600px-Reznorexoticbirds.jpg
Image 79
https://i.discogs.com/QtJoZtsjg9kHpeLThQ0FFy6aWfQnGamZOmFEf_ZEdsw/rs:fit/g:sm/q:90/h:502/w:500/czM6Ly9kaX
Njb2dz/LWRhdGFiYXNILWlt/YWdlcy9SLTk1MjMy/MC0xMTc2NzM0ODEw/LmpwZWc.jpeg
Image 81
roanokefestival.com/blog/wp-
content/uploads/2018/04/29244404_1603820049654617_3389582890013556736_n.jpgmain.jpg
Image 83
www.edwinknip.com/Hoesjes/Earring/lp/kGE-LP-Source8314-USAA.jpg
Image 84
encrypted-
tbn0.gstatic.com/images?q=tbn:ANd9GcRdbMOLU7ZxMboR4HrAghshSmm9eTbw4NiVtwCccmE3Nha2EHhFjTIPHwtfbt52
KBqrZ_0&usqp=CAU
Image 85
www.discogs.com/release/13529614-The-Pretenders-The-Pretenders-Concert/image/SW1hZ2U6Mzk3ODIwMDE=

Image 86

i.discogs.com/OwE1zJmODN0tckPMADqeZXAmcKAcWvfSDlKKfmQXFb0/rs:fill/g:sm/q:40/h:300/w:300/czM6Ly9kaXNjb2
dz/LWRhdGFiYXNILWlt/YWdlcy9SLTE1NzE1/MTk4LTE1OTY0NTc4/MjAtNTkzMi5qcGVn.jpeg

Image 87

www.umojaproductions.com/Assets/Images/JoelSolloway1.jpg

Image 88A

https://i.prcdn.co/img?regionKey=xbZfPECo7XnwBEP8IWpWzA%3D%3D

Image 89

people.com/thmb/JK6tFG13i_4LFA1puY4hiYqzkbg=/750x0/filters:no_upscale():max_bytes(150000):strip_icc():focal(149x
0:151x2):format(webp)/patrick-stewart-300-3-12a3854019d3457aa5350839423eb5fc.jpg

Image 90

encrypted-tbn1.gstatic.com/images?q=tbn:ANd9GcSQR_zNilDr742JPfw6PsUlikukrkmbNp7Paz21zjiHT-86hL-C

Image 91

i.ebayimg.com/images/g/gaoAAOSwmetcnIF0/s-l1600.jpg

Image 91A

i.ebayimg.com/images/g/UREAAOSwXcljhtOC/s-l1600.jpg

Image 94

encrypted-tbn3.gstatic.com/images?q=tbn:ANd9GcS6L5ypCcHFYSlD1LwGufxl4OT8FtJ9cRzO6_p2a6kHwgTc6LZM

Image 95

upload.wikimedia.org/wikipedia/commons/7/77/Spitzer_logo.png

Image 95A

https://i.ebayimg.com/images/g/PesAAOSw1hhk7zSv/s-l1200.webp

Image 96A and Image 124

iconape.com/wp-content/png_logo_vector/hgtv.png

Image 96

images-na.ssl-images-amazon.com/images/S/pv-target-
images/37bb09b4915af8723b9654c13ac23e1eab38ab33e8b56368f98220fb6bc88000._RI_TTW_SX1080_FMwebp_.jpg

Image 98

youtu.be/cASeFxeTRPc?feature=shared

Image 99

https://encrypted-
tbn2.gstatic.com/images?q=tbn:ANd9GcSBC70_h6W2drnC6hfha9xsVr6tjMnonebTF_NhVuZd9pp0gROX

Image 103

images.genius.com/78d722cdc085d3e903ef524af5f5cedf.283x283x1.jpg

Image 104

i5.walmartimages.com/seo/Dirty-Dancing-Soundtrack-CD_291983c0-dff9-455e-9ec6-
d2f6238af131_1.da536a612e452321c34deb25efb45864.jpeg?odnHeight=160&odnWidth=160&odnBg=FFFFF

Image 108

cdn.commercialcafe.com/images/145595CA-5AD7-4A89-85F7-FFF03D4D45B4/1171739.jpg?height=675

Image 113A

https://putinbay.com/wp-content/uploads/2018/11/pib_airport.jpg

Image 114

media.cleveland.com/popmusic_impact/photo/11409154-large.jpg

Image 115 and Image 116

s3-media0.fl.yelpcdn.com/bphoto/GMTjzUqzHG6aXC-XpTT8pA/348s.jpg

Image 124 and Image 96A

https://cdn.freebiesupply.com/logos/large/2x/hgtv-1-logo-svg-vector.svg

Image 126

live.staticflickr.com/1237/527386892_342c6cea27_b.jpg

Image 126A

https://pbs.twimg.com/media/EcQTC9RWoAEeUjz?format=jpg&name=medium

Image 127

cdn.freebiesupply.com/logos/large/2x/cleveland-cavs-logo-png-transparent.png

Image 128

cdn.freebiesupply.com/images/large/2x/orlando-magic-logo-transparent.png

Image 129

media.bizj.us/view/img/6281481/denver-nuggets-logo*900xx2000-1125-0-434.jpg

Image 130

upload.wikimedia.org/wikipedia/en/thumb/0/02/Washington_Wizards_logo.svg/400px-
Washington_Wizards_logo.svg.png

Image 132

onthisday.com/images/people/bob-hope.jpg?w=360

Image 133

youtu.be/cDDWvj_q-o8?feature=shared

Image 135

i.ytimg.com/vi/a7VLvGyZ9B8/hqdefault.jpg

Image 136
youtu.be/3GJ4kM-Aqec?feature=shared
Image 137 and Image 137A
passporttosandiego.com/wp-content/uploads/2016/04/uss-miway-halographic.jpg
Image 138 and Image 138A
piccoloexplorer.com/wp-content/uploads/2021/09/USS-Midway-Museum-San-Diego-with-Kids-683x1024.jpg
Image 139
static.wixstatic.com/media/aa1934_8ac234f59947427b8987b044ad6d9339~mv2.jpg/v1/fill/w_1440,h_812,fp_0.50_0.5
0,q_85,enc_auto/aa1934_8ac234f59947427b8987b044ad6d9339~mv2.jpg
Image 140
ir.4sqi.net/img/general/original/NXSMX4F4T5C2N3FDLN2X4DWPAGRVGG4TZPKRJEIPP2FG4KJH.jpg
Image 141
weekendwanderer2016.files.wordpress.com/2018/12/hyde-park-trails.jpg?w=584
Image 142
hudsonrivervalley.com/destinations/images/01Study.jpg
Image 143
res.cloudinary.com/dktp1ybbx/image/upload/c_limit,h_170,w_170/f_auto,fl_lossy,q_auto/v1648660403/organization/
prod/1211041/HZgNgcZANQ.jpg
Image 144
stewarthaasracing.com/wp-content/uploads/aspen-dental.gif
Image 145
seeklogo.com/images/S/signet-jewelers-logo-863B80ED62-seeklogo.com.png
Image 146
https://encrypted-tbn0.gstatic.com/images?q=tbn:ANd9GcQcFo7WOaEhkPzTgvxACgQib1-cnxncT87dZlsQNeVSG2-
qhxKbEJqa4hmAjQSOes8rYck&usqp=CAU
Image 147
media-cdn.tripadvisor.com/media/photo-s/04/62/e2/d9/union-oyster-house.jpg
Image 148
a.mktgcdn.com/p/XKuxm74MVaiMVvk8946L44kcrLOxKfyHWn13Za5gGBs/1429x1429.jpg
Image 149
canoeclubwinebar.com/wp-content/uploads/2022/08/jerry.jpg
Image 155
scontent-ord5-1.xx.fbcdn.net/v/t1.18169-9/295300_330774516999684_1068299268_n.jpg?_nc_cat=111&ccb=1-
7&_nc_sid=cdbe9c&_nc_ohc=g_3lRYY-2pwAX_KGvlt&_nc_ht=scontent-ord5-
1.xx&oh=00_AfAzanMXXQzDDzSr_hFd7zHlyuK5t6TAXJXwV_mMPw4pBQ&oe=650DDA24
Image 156
d10j3mvrs1suex.cloudfront.net/s:bzglfiles/u/39737/cacc00d89478b889d8e07bcf587fad1eefb64b55/original/RR_053.jpg
/!!/b%3AW1sicmVzaXplIiwxODAwXSxblm1heCJdLFsid2UiXV0%3D/meta%3AeyJzcmNCdWNrZXQiOiJiemdsZmlsZXMifQ%
3D%3D.jpg
Image 157
tasteoflakewood.com/wp-content/uploads/2022/05/live-music-jeff-varga.jpg
Image 164
https://encrypted-tbn2.gstatic.com/images?q=tbn:ANd9GcQufMv7GlFipeY7wvOS2RN203cmNTzu3-Dzfl78ccSjtvsDbR7s
Image 165
images.squarespace-cdn.com/content/v1/5e7503d14749db7726b38512/56863282-283c-494f-8a7a-
5248e4b23ee4/DF+Logo+Color+HQ.png?format=1500w
Image 166
worldmedicalinnovation.org/wp-content/uploads/2023/07/3O1A5055-1024x683.jpg
Image 167
upload.wikimedia.org/wikipedia/en/1/1d/Brotherhood_of_Locomotive_Engineers_and_Trainmen_logo.jpg
Image 171
https://scontent-ord5-2.xx.fbcdn.net/v/t1.18169-
9/297303_10150389056089795_52009867_n.jpg?stp=c159.0.643.643a_dst-jpg_s851x315&_nc_cat=102&ccb=1-
7&_nc_sid=da31f3&_nc_ohc=QF2ptfeACKcAX8hTsuc&_nc_ht=scontent-ord5-
2.xx&oh=00_AfDKnT_X2aUxMpc_9W0_fwubRraHJr0AuI7nDGh-X3FCog&oe=650E0209
Image 172
scontent-ord5-2.xx.fbcdn.net/v/t31.18172-
8/18891749_1424858837557679_5905880711994612431_o.jpg?stp=c205.0.1638.1638a_dst-
jpg_s851x315&_nc_cat=110&ccb=1-7&_nc_sid=da31f3&_nc_ohc=2OF7qSqO-8UAX9Fn32T&_nc_ht=scontent-ord5-
2.xx&oh=00_AfBxrKAjS_EECOmbpWoFoU2fkG4_43m9wfh0gP3LhKUH9w&oe=650DCE13
image of George on front flap by
Barb Pennington Studio

All images including logos, albums, photos, illustrations or drawing in this book are used under the Fair use law. The Fair use in the United States is a law that permits limited use of copyrighted material without having to first acquire permission from the copyright holder. Fair use is one of the limitations to copyright law intended to balance the interests of copyright holders with the public interest in the wider distribution and use of creative works for editorial purposes. You don't need to ask permission if the copyrighted material used will educate, inform, or express opinion protected under the Constitution's First Amendment.

Logos

The logos used have been previously published or publicly displayed outside of this book and sources have been listed. The entire logo is used to convey the meaning intended and avoid tarnishing or misrepresenting the intended image. The logo is of a size and resolution sufficient to maintain the quality intended by the company or organization. The significance of the logo is to help the reader identify the organization as described in this book. Use of the logo in the book complies with guidelines, and fair use under United States copyright law as described by the above rationale. The logos used in this book educate, inform, or express opinion protected under the Constitution's First Amendment.

Albums

The album covers used been previously published or publicly displayed outside of this book and sources have been listed. The entire album cover is used because it is a form of product packaging, the entire image is needed to identify the product, properly convey the meaning and branding intended, and avoid tarnishing or misrepresenting the image. Use for this purpose does not compete with the purposes of the original artwork, namely the artist's providing graphic design services to music concerns, and in turn marketing music to the public. The significance of the visual is solely to illustrate the audio recording in question, and help the reader know they have the correct item as reflected in this book. Use of the Album cover in the book complies with guidelines, and fair use under United States copyright law as described by the above rationale. The Album covers used in this book educate, inform, or express opinion protected under the Constitution's First Amendment.

Photos, Illustrations or Drawings

The photos, illustrations or drawings used have been previously published or publicly displayed outside of this book and sources have been listed. The significance of the photos, illustrations or drawings are solely to illustrate the person, place or thing as reflected in this book, and help the reader know they have the correct person, place or thing that is being talked about in this book. Use for this purpose does not compete with the purposes of the original photo. Use of the photo in the book complies with guidelines, and fair use under United States copyright law as described by the above rationale. The photos, illustrations and drawings used in this book educate, inform, or express opinions protected under the Constitution's First Amendment.

Music Resources:

Just in case you want to listen,
Here are some URL's for the music talked about in the book:

Cleveland Clinic *Empathy*:
https://www.youtube.com/watch?v=cDDWvj_q-o8

American Noise *Anyone With A Heart* (Live):
https://www.youtube.com/watch?v=I1BtAzMdUns

American Noise *Runnin Through The Night*:
https://www.youtube.com/watch?v=ZHJlvKtMcAo

Eric Carmen *Hungry Eyes*:
https://www.youtube.com/watch?v=2ssCL292DQA

Eric Carmen *Never Gonna Fall In Love Again*:
https://www.youtube.com/watch?v=POkE9eI23cU

I-X Indoor Amusement Park Jingle:
https://www.youtube.com/watch?v=rQtYemx9GLQ

1-800-General:
https://www.youtube.com/watch?v=KtY9S6NCaQ4

Spitzer *85th Anniversary*:
https://www.youtube.com/watch?v=FpYCxC3Azgs

USA Insulation:
https://www.youtube.com/watch?v=jOYHnGRsMog

Finding Aliza:
https://www.youtube.com/watch?v=cASeFxeTRPc

Exotic Birds:
https://www.youtube.com/watch?v=t40zLgIYxXY

Giorgio's Oven Fresh Pizza Company:
https://www.youtube.com/watch?v=ZL9PBDtvfCo

Bridges
https://www.youtube.com/watch?v=Asw_xZis2Ps

Monica Robins Whiskey Kings *Bobby McGee*:
https://www.youtube.com/watch?v=IohL5uXhSrE

Georgia *Tonight*:
https://www.youtube.com/watch?v=Bm9hiFkhHjk

Those Guys:
https://www.facebook.com/100054343364768/videos/663981031130315

Club Wow (synthesizer) *the Nights Are So Long*
https://www.youtube.com/watch?v=HSqaw2hYByA

Fayrewether *Everything's OK*:
https://www.youtube.com/watch?v=UeHGqGwtYqk

Euclid Beach Band *No Surf In Cleveland*:
https://www.youtube.com/watch?v=dozcurR0hx0

www.ingramcontent.com/pod-product-compliance
Lightning Source LLC
Chambersburg PA
CBHW050717150726
48196CB00029B/832/J